Wellington Squadrons

IN FOCUS

**RED
KITE**

Acknowledgements

Most of the photos in this book have come from the Simon Parry Collection and www.ww2images.com. The publishers would like to thank Andy Thomas for generously filling in the gaps from his own collection where possible. Further books in the series are planned, if you have any photos that you think might be suitable, especially of RAF Bomber Command, please contact the publishers.

Printed in England by Cromwell Press Group.

Wellington Squadrons
IN FOCUS
by
Paul Freer and Simon Parry

Other titles in this series;

Lancaster Squadrons in Focus
Beaufighter Squadrons in Focus
Hampden Squadrons in Focus
Mosquito Squadrons in Focus Pt 1
Hurricane Squadrons in Focus Pt 1
Czechs in the RAF in Focus
B-17 Groups of the 8th AF in Focus
B-24 Groups of the 8th AF in Focus
Dornier 17 in Focus

Wellington Squadrons in Focus
ISBN 9780955473548

First published 2009 by
Red Kite
PO Box 223,
Walton on Thames
Surrey, KT12 3YQ

All books can be purchased online at
www.redkitebooks.co.uk

Designed by Mark Postlethwaite and
Simon Parry

"Moosemen" of 419 Squadron quite at home in the snow at Mildenhall, 9th February 1942. From left to right: S/Ldr F.W.S Turner; P/O K.E.Hobson; F/Sgt G.P.Fowler; F/Sgt C.A.Robson; F/Sgt N.G.Arthur; F/Sgt H.T.Dell. Tragically, after completing his tour with this crew, F/Sgt Dell volunteered for one more sortie with the C/O, Wing Commander "Moose" Fulton, and was killed along with his C/O on the way back from Hamburg on the night of 28/29th July 1942.

Contents

The Vickers Wellington

The Vickers-Armstrong Wellington was a truly remarkable aeroplane. Designed to an Air Ministry specification for a day bomber originally issued in 1932, the Wellington entered Royal Air Force service in October 1938 and did not finally retire from RAF service until March 1953. The Wellington carried out its first operational sortie on the very day that war was declared, when nine aircraft of Nos.37 and 149 Squadrons carried out an armed reconnaissance of the Schilling Roads. It was the only British bomber to be operational throughout World War Two, and the only British medium bomber to serve in all major theatres of the war. The Wellington was produced in greater numbers than any other British bomber, with a total of 11,461 examples being built (the Lancaster was a distant second with 7,377 being constructed), and the only British bomber to remain in production throughout the war.

K4049, the daddy of them all, crossing the River Wey at Brooklands via the toll bridge; aircraft bearing RAF roundels were exempt of the toll!

L4212, the Wellington MkI prototype at Brooklands.

Originally designed as a medium bomber, the Wellington went on to serve in the anti-submarine role; as a torpedo bomber; an electronic counter-measures platform; a paratroop drop aircraft; minesweeper; transport; and training aeroplane, not to mention numerous experimental versions. Ultimately, the Wellington was to be powered by four different engine types – Bristol Pegasus, Rolls Royce Merlin, Pratt & Whitney Twin Wasp and the Bristol Hercules – almost doubling in power output from the 915hp Bristol Pegasus that powered the prototype to the 1,735 hp Bristol Hercules of the late-war anti-submarine variants. And all this from an airframe that was effectively obsolete before it even entered service.

Unlike any of its contemporaries, the Wellington did not employ the stressed skin method of construction by that time finding favour with other aircraft manufacturers. Instead, in order to utilise the most powerful engines then available and yet still keep within the strict tare weight specified by the Air Ministry, Vickers-Armstrong opted for the 'geodetic' method of construction pioneered by their structures designer, Barnes Wallis. This method of construction comprised a metal latticework of stress-equalising members covered in doped fabric, and had been successfully utilised by Wallis in his airship designs and subsequently on the Wellesley aircraft.

The geodetic construction possessed the airframe of great structural strength, and the fabric covering was less susceptible to damage than the stressed metal skin of other bomber aircraft. Time and time again the Wellington would prove

Above: The legendary geodetic structure of the wings.

Right: View from the nose prior to the the installation of the turret, the pilot's seat and the control yoke have already been fitted. These two items were installed as a complete sub-assembly.

itself capable of sustaining extensive combat damage and still return to base, a quality that endeared the aircraft to the aircrews. A less attractive characteristic of the geodetic construction was its flexibility, which caused the whole airframe to flex in flight and to wobble alarmingly when taxiing.

In other respects, the Wellington was strange mix of old and new technologies. The fuel tanks were located in the wings which, as well as increasing structural strength, also had the advantage of maximising space within the fuselage for the crew stations, bomb bay and ancillary equipment. The Wellington was fitted with Frise ailerons and featured a number of cutting edge aircraft systems, including a hydraulically operated retractable undercarriage, split trailing edge flaps and bomb bay doors. However, early examples lacked armour protection and self-sealing fuel tanks, the absence of which would prove very costly in early operations. The earliest production examples also lacked power operated gun turrets, although these were introduced before the Wellington commenced its operational career.

This then was the aircraft that would become the mainstay of Bomber Command in the early years of the war, and would go to serve with many squadrons of the Allied air forces. Versatile, immensely strong, easy to fly and much loved by air and ground crew alike, the Wellington was a classic of its generation. This book is gratefully dedicated to all those who designed, built, maintained and flew in this remarkable aircraft.

Early Wellingtons on the Brooklands production line. These examples have the Vickers designed manually operated front turret which soon proved to be wholly ineffective and was replaced by the power operated Fraser Nash FN5A turret.

Covering the fuselage with fabric. The fabric was attached to wooden stringers fixed to the geodetic structure using over 8,000 tiny screws, which in turn were covered by strips of doped fabric. No less than nine coats of cellulose dope were then applied to tighten and weather-proof the fabric before finishing off with the camouflage scheme.

From the inside

Above and Right: Two views of the instrument panel of a Wellington MkI – subsequent variants differed only very slightly. Behind the control yoke can be seen the 'Basic Six' flying instruments common to all RAF aircraft of the period. The panel to the right of this contains the engine instruments and undercarriage controls, below which is the P-Type compass in its bracket mounting.

Below: An unusual view of the pilot and second pilot of a 75 Squadron Wellington, taken looking up through the entrance hatch under the nose of the aircraft. Occupying the pilot's seat, wearing his trademark white flying overalls, is Wg Cdr Kay DFC, then C/O of 75 Squadron.

"What do you mean we're lost!" A concerned pilot checks up on his navigator, whereas a fellow crewmember takes a rest blissfully unaware of the situation. This shot shows just how much equipment was carried in operational Wellingtons. The black cylinders lining the upper fuselage are oxygen cylinders. The semicircular padding on the port side of the fuselage is the steadying frame used when taking sextant shots from the astrodome directly above, the identical frame on the starboard side is also just visible below the rope stowage.

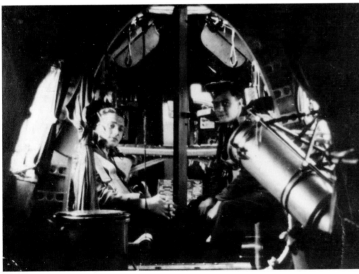

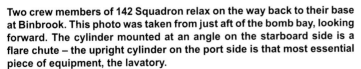

Two crew members of 142 Squadron relax on the way back to their base at Binbrook. This photo was taken from just aft of the bomb bay, looking forward. The cylinder mounted at an angle on the starboard side is a flare chute – the upright cylinder on the port side is that most essential piece of equipment, the lavatory.

This view, taken from further back in the fuselage, shows the construction of the Wellington to advantage. The geodetic members and structural frame were constructed from a light alloy and were both left unpainted. Above the geodetic framework can be seen the wooden stringers to which the fabric was attached. Although the fabric was white when first attached the airframe, the application of successive coats of dope turned the fabric to a brick red colour, hence the dark appearance in this photo.

Above Left: The Frazer Nash FN10 rear turret on a Wellington MkIc, fitted with two 0.303 machine guns. The rearward opening doors enabled the gunner to abandon the aircraft in an emergency by simply rotating the turret to one side and falling backwards into the airflow, a 'luxury' not enjoyed by any other crew member. Later variants of the Wellington would be equipped with the much improved FN4 or FN120 turrets, both of which were equipped with four 0.303 machine guns.

Above: The Frazer Nash FN5A front turret was standard on every bomber variant except the early MkIs. Although this hydraulically operated turret was a significant improvement on the original Vickers manually operated design of the MkI, it still did not provide sufficient protection to enable the Wellington to operate in daylight and was of little value as a defence against night-fighters.

Left: The interior of the Frazer Nash FN10 rear turret, fitted to some early variants of the Wellington (Mks Ia, Ic, II and GRVIII). The turret is equipped with two 0.303 Browning machine guns, the elevation for which is provided by the hydraulic rams immediately outboard of the guns. The turret controls are side mounted, directly above the ammunition trays, with the reflector gunsight centrally located on a V-shaped frame between the guns.

Lineage

Above: The prototype K4049 clearly identifiable without any form of defensive turrets. The other main differences between the prototype and the MkI were a narrower fuselage in the prototype and the fairings on the undercarriage, which were removed on all production versions.

L4212, the MkI prototype. The main recognition feature of the MkI (as opposed to the MkIa) was the early Vickers gun turrets in the nose and tail. These were soon found to be inferior to the Fraser-Nash built versions which replaced them at the RAF's request from the MkIa onwards.

L4250, the MkII prototype. This airframe was a basic MkIa (note the Fraser-Nash turrets) but powered by inline Merlin Xs.

P9238 was the MkIII production prototype. The MkIII was fitted with the more powerful Hercules engines. Visual differences between the MkIa and the MkIII are the cut-out section behind the nose turret, (introduced on the MkIc) an extra intake on top of the engines and the more powerful FN20 four gun rear turret. A distinguishing feature on all Hercules powered versions was the location of the exhausts on the inboard side of the engine nacelle.

R1625 shown here is a MkIV. This variant was visually similar to other marks but was fitted with American Pratt and Whitney Twin Wasp engines. The key difference visually is the origin of the exhaust pipes which on the MkIV appeared under the cooling gills and on the outboard side of the engine nacelle.

The MkX was the most produced of all Wellington variants with over 3800 being built. Main recognition feature was the extended intakes on top of the engines and the large spinners carried by most MkXs.

The MkX airframe was converted for maritime operations into three main variants. The MkXII seen here and latterly the MkXIV had the ASV MkIII radar internally mounted in the nose and a Leigh Light installed under the fuselage.

The other development of the MkX was the MkXIII (seen here) which had ASV MkII radar fitted requiring four sets of aerials along the rear fuselage and two under the wings. These aircraft sometimes operated in the torpedo bomber role.

A Wellington MkVIII fitted with the ASV MkII aerials on the fuselage. The main difference between the MkVIII and the MkXIII was the engines, Pegasus for the former and Hercules for the latter.

"Sticklebacks" and "Goofingtons"

Air to Surface Vessel radar (ASV) played a significant role in the maritime air war. Developed in parallel with Airborne Interception radar, ASV was first demonstrated in trials in 1938. The first operational ASV sets (ASV Mk1) were fitted to Hudson and Sunderland aircraft of Coastal Command but were only capable of looking directly forward and consequently were of limited value.

The first ASV to be fitted to Wellingtons was the sideways-looking ASV MKII, sometimes known as Long Range Air to Surface Vessel radar (LRASV). In trials at the Royal Aircraft Establishment (RAE), aircraft flying at 2,000ft ASL detected a 10,000 ton ship at 40 miles range, a destroyer at 20 miles and a submarine at 8 miles.

ASV MkII required the installation of four antennae on each side of the rear fuselage and a further four antennae on the spine of the rear fuselage. Wellingtons so equipped included the GR VIII, GR XI, GR XII and GR XIII variants and were known as "Sticklebacks" or, to the crews on Malta, as "Goofingtons". Combined with Yagi antennae beneath the wings and lower nose of the aircraft, ASV MKII provided the radar operator with information on both range and bearing of surface vessels.

The introduction of ASV significantly increased sightings of U-boats. Not only did this result in the occasional sinking of U-boats, it forced submarines below surface during the vital process of replenishing their batteries. This reduced the effectiveness of U-boats and, indirectly, reduced the number of attacks on Allied shipping. Aircraft equipped with ASV MkII proved so successful at detecting submarines that, in August 1942, the Germans introduced the "Metox" receiver to warn of approaching aircraft equipped with ASV.

In late 1942, a new version of ASV was introduced, the MkIII. This was a centimetric radar, comparable with the H2S navigation radar used by Bomber Command. The "Stickleback" and Yagi antennae were replaced by a single rotating scanner housed in a radome beneath the nose of the aircraft, which in turn necessitated the replacement of the front gun turret with a Perspex cupola. Wellingtons equipped with ASV MkIII included late production GR XI's GRXIIs and the GRXIV.

ASV MkIII remained effective until the end of the war and, in calm seas, was even capable of detecting a 'schnorkel' device from a submerged submarine. It was not until the closing months of the war that the Germans introduced 'Naxos', a warning receiver operating on centimetric wavelengths. Even then, Naxos had a maximum range of just 5,000 metres; in other words, less than one minute's warning of an attack.

Equipped with ASV, Wellington squadrons played a significant role in the Battle of the Atlantic and in defeating the U-boat menace in other theatres of operation.

Another MkVIII but this time experimentally fitted with the nose mounted ASV MkIII radar removing the need for the external aerials.

The Weird and the Wonderful!

L4250 experimental aircraft with a cannon for a mid-upper.

L4250 and the turret again, but now she has grown a twin tail!

Z8416/G the 'G' indicated that the aircraft should be guarded at all times - perhaps this explains why the wire fence is in this very rare photo! The big secret here is the 40mm cannon that can just be picked out in the trees. The 'lump' above the cockpit is a covered sighting position.

The MkVI was designed to be a high altitude bomber, complete with a pressurised crew cabin. However, problems with the extreme cold at high altitude delayed the development of the project and the few examples built were soon replaced by the more versatile Mosquito.

The Whittle jet engine test-bed at Bruntingthorpe in 1944.

The Squadrons

149 Squadron Wellingtons over Paris
on Bastille Day, 1939.

8 SQUADRON

India
Dec 43 to May 45

Code Letters
None

Operational bases:
Khormaksar
12/43 - 5/45
Disbanded

A member of No.8 Squadron salutes the cameraman from the cockpit of a Wellington GR XIII, at Salalah, February 1944. The GR XIII was a dedicated maritime patrol variant, fitted with Hercules XVII engines rated at 1,175hp for low altitude operations. Just visible on the rear fuselage are the 'stickleback' antennae for the ASV Mk II radar.

Ground crew salvage spare parts from a GR XIII of No 8. Squadron that crash-landed at Bardas Kassim, 1944. The rear of the aircraft appears to have taken the brunt of the impact, although the open escape hatch above the cockpit suggests that the crew in the forward positions got out safely.

Although dedicated to the maritime patrol role, early GR XIIIs retained the standard bomber colour scheme.

The structure projecting above the pilot's windscreen is not an original part of the aircraft!

Servicing Far Eastern style, the ground crews, used to working in the biting wind and rain in England, encountered new hazards and new wildlife when they arrived in the Far East.

Code Letters
KA
WS

Operational bases:
Stradishall 1/39 7/39
Honington 7/39 - 8/42
Waddington 8/42 - 9/42
Re-equipped with
Lancasters

Below: Wellington MkIc T2468 WS-Y –Yorker at Honington, August 1940. 'Yorker' had a remarkably long career, completing 13 operations with IX Squadron before going on to serve with 75, 40 and 311 Squadrons. Operations complete, T2468 then served with a number of Operational Training Units until being SOC in April 1944.

Above: Smiles all round as groundcrew of IX Squadron gather in front of Mk III WS-Z at Honington, in 1941. "Zola" is an early example of the widespread practice in IX Squadron of naming aircraft based upon the individual identification letter. "Zola" was the girlfriend of Buck Ryan, the eponymous hero of the popular Daily Mirror cartoon of the time. This practice was continued when the squadron converted to Lancasters, perhaps the most well-known being centurion W4964 WS-J "Johnny Walker".

No.9 Squadron in formation before the war.

German Officers inspect the fuselage of WS-L (R3220) which came down on the outskirts of Ostend returning from Dusseldorf on the night of 7/8th December 1940 Surprisingly, nobody has 'souvenired' the fuselage roundel yet, a common fate for fallen fabric covered Wellingtons!

Flt Lt James Cowan RNZAF in front of an anonymous Wellington MkIc at a rain-swept Honington, circa early 1942. Sadly, after completing at least 27 operations with IX Squadron and earning a DFC, James Cowan was killed in a flying accident in March 1943 when his 1661 HCU Lancaster crashed near Newark-upon-Trent following an engine fire.

Flt Lt Cowan again, this time with MkIII X3794 WS-V "Barbara Mary". This aircraft later transferred to No.75 Squadron and was one of two aircraft lost, both from that squadron, from a small force of eleven aircraft attacking Emden on the night of 3rd/4th September 1942.

F/Lt Cowan and crew pose with "Pam", a WAAF MT driver, in front of "Barbara Mary". The crew, L-R, are P/O L.J.Brown: Sgt J.F.Harrison: F/Lt J.Cowan: Sgt J.A. Talbot: Sgt R.W.Brown. This crew were fortunate to escape with only minor injuries when, briefed to attack Emden on the night 6/7th June 1942, they crash-landed a different V-Victor (Z1575) shortly after take-off from Honington.

Down in the desert

Having completed a number of sorties against German targets as an Observer with IX Squadron, Sgt Alan Butler volunteered to serve in the Middle East. On the 20th March 1941, Butler set out with his new crew to attempt an unprecedented non-stop transit to the airfield at Benina, near Benghazi on the North African coast. They didn't quite make it. Emerging on dead-reckoning from cloud cover and with fuel running low, the decision was made to a make a landing on the first land to come into view. This turned out to be a beach in enemy held territory, where the crew managed to set fire to their aircraft just before enemy soldiers arrived on the scene. The crew were soon captured and taken to Tripoli for interrogation.

Right: Soldiers of the Afrika Corps inspect the burnt-out Wellington.

Below: The complete crew being driven away to spend the rest of the war in captivity. The front gunner, Sgt Bill Ainsbury, is seated 3rd left facing the camera whilst the Observer, Alan Butler, sits with his back to the camera.

Below right: Mussolini's 'gateway to Tripoli' forms the backdrop to this carefully composed picture as the second pilot, Sgt Alan Millington, converses with his captors.

12 SQUADRON

Bomber Command
July 40 to Nov 42

Code Letters
PH

Operational bases:
Binbrook 7/40 9/42
Wickenby 9/42 - 11/42
Re-equipped with
Lancasters

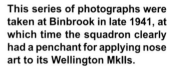

This series of photographs were taken at Binbrook in late 1941, at which time the squadron clearly had a penchant for applying nose art to its Wellington MkIIs.

Above: P/O Barnes looks down from the cockpit of "St.George", with four sortie markings depicted as shields bearing the cross of St.George.

Left: Wg Cdr Roberts, the squadron CO, and crew stand somewhat self-consciously in front a Wellington II adorned with nose art in the form of a ram on a shield. The Merlin engine of the MkII was longer than the Pegasus fitted to the MkI, and consequently the propeller arc was moved forward to a position in line with the pilot's sliding window. This aircraft is one of those fitted with an additional internal bar to this window.

In contrast to their CO, Sqn Ldr Baxter and crew strike an altogether more relaxed pose in front of "Joyous!", another of the unit's MkIIs. The demarcation between the top surface camouflage colour and the night undersurface is much lower on this aircraft. This 'halfway' style was applied for a brief period in summer 1940.

"V-Victory" demonstrates the later camouflage demarcation high up on the fuselage. This aircraft, W5376, was another to have a remarkably long operational life, going on to serve with 104 Squadron in North Africa and Malta before finally being lost in June 1943.

More 12 Squadron nose art, this time from W5430, the "Spirit of Notts", which crash-landed on return from Cologne on the 30th July 1941. The association with Robin Hood, his "merry" men and the scoreboard in pints of beer are obvious, but the winking owl less so - possibly a reference to the wisdom of an experienced crew or, more likely, the oft-quoted bomber crew expression "Only Owls and Bloody Fools Fly at Night". The meaning of the individual letters on some of the pint glasses is unknown.

An interesting fact

The squadron converted from the Fairey Battle to the Merlin-engined Wellington MkII, and then later converted straight onto the Avro Lancaster. The squadron was therefore one of the few in Bomber Command to operate solely on Merlin engined aircraft throughout World War II, doubling the number of engines per aircraft each time it converted.

A good example of the sturdiness of the Wellington. Taken following a crash-landing at Binbrook in July 1941 when with 12 Squadron, W5358 was repaired and went on to serve with 158 Squadron, eventually being hit by flak and abandoned by P/O McMillan RNZAF and crew near Cologne on the night of 12/13th April 1942.

Wellington MkII W5381 which crashed 18th June 1942 on a night flying test.

PH-N tucks her undercarriage up after take off in 1942, note the later style fuselage windows and the revised lower visibility roundels introduced in May 1942.

A tale of two Wellingtons

The squadron suffered a most unusual double loss on the night of 26-27 March 1942 during a raid on Essen, when two of the Squadron's Wellington IIs were shot down over Holland by the Messerschmitt Bf110 of night-fighter ace Oblt. Prinz Egmont zur Lippe-Weissenfeld of 5/NJG2. The Wellingtons, W5371 and W5372, had been built consecutively on the Vickers production line and had been delivered to the squadron on the same day, only to be lost within an hour each other at the hands of the same opponent.

W5360 at Binbrook which was lost as PH-U on an op to Brest 6/7 July 1941.

14
SQUADRON
Coastal Command
Nov 44 to May 45

Code Letters
CX

Operational bases:
Chivenor 11/44 - 5/45
Disbanded

Having previously flown the Martin Marauder on bombing missions in Italy, No.14 Squadron reformed at Chivenor in October 1944 in the anti-submarine role equipped with the Wellington GRXIV.

Above: A GRXIV at St Merryn 28th April 1945.

Right: Clearing the snow from a Wellington needed a steady nerve and sturdy boots!

Below: One of the unit's Wellington GRXIVs is seen here at Chivenor late in 1944. Having previously flown the high-performance Martin Marauder, the conversion to the lumbering Wellington must have been an interesting experience for the Squadron's pilots. The GR XIV was a dedicated anti-submarine variant, and this example shows to advantage the ASV III radar in the tear-drop fairing under the nose and, immediately to the rear of the open bomb bay, the retracted Leigh Light.

15

SQUADRON
Bomber Command
May 40 to Apr 41

Code Letters
LS

Operational bases:
Wyton 5/40 - 4/41
Re-equipped with
Stirlings

Above: T2961 LS-S with quite elaborate nose-art at Wyton in 1941. She went on to join 18 OTU and was lost on the night of 14th March 1942 when she crashed into trees on take off at Bramcote.

Above: Wellington LS-W at Wyton early in the war.

Left: Wellington GRXIV RW-D of 36 Squadron at Benbecula in the Outer Hebrides early in 1945. Although the aircraft appears to be painted white overall, the standard camouflage applied to anti-submarine GRXIVs included disruptive camouflage on the upper surfaces of the wings and tailplane, with a narrow strip of disruptive camouflage along the spine.

24
SQUADRON
Transport
Feb 43 to Jan 44

Code Letters
NQ

Operational bases:
Hendon 2/43 - 1/44

Points of Interest

24 Squadron flew a miscellany of aircraft types in the transport role, including American-built Curtiss SBC- 2 Helldiver biplanes originally intended for the French Air Force.

"Duke of Cornwall", a Wellington CMkXV of 24 Squadron at Hendon in 1942 or early 1943. The Wellington CMkXV was an interim solution to the desperate shortage of transport aircraft available to the RAF in the early part of World War II, pending the arrival of dedicated transport types such as the Dakota. The conversion to the transport role was achieved by adapting selected MkIa airframes, including the removal of nose, tail and ventral turrets and the installation of a door midway down the starboard rear fuselage. N2990 seen here is typical of such aircraft, having previously served in standard MkIa bomber configuration as 'P' with 115 Squadron and then with 11 OTU before being converted to the transport role. In common with several other aircraft in the squadron, N2990 has dummy nose and tail turrets painted on the faired-in fuselage to create the illusion that the aircraft was armed. After a varied career lasting nearly four years, in which this one airframe had unusually seen service as a front-line bomber, trainer and transport aircraft, N2990 was eventually SOC on the 19th March 1943.

Above: A 36 Sqn MkXIV in Italy and Below: 36 Squadron line up for a formal photo

36
SQUADRON
Middle East
Oct 42 to Sept 44

Coastal Command
Sept 44 to June 45

Code Letters
RW

Operational bases:
Tanjore 10/42 - 4/43
Dhabalia 4/43 - 6/43
Blida 6/43 - 4/44
Reghaia 4/44 - 9/44
Tarquinia 9/44

Chivenor 9/44 - 3/45
Benbecula 3/45 6/45
Disbanded

Code Letters
LF

Middle East
Nov 40 to Oct 44

Operational bases:
Feltwell 5/39 - 11/40
Luqa 11/40 - 12/40
Fayid 12/40
Shallufa 12/40 - 4/42
LG09 4/42 - 6/42
LG224 6/42
Abu Sueir 6/42 - 11/42
LG224 11/42
LG106 11/42
LG140 11/42 - 1/43
Benina 1/43
El Magrum 1/43 - 2/43
Gardabia 2/43 - 5/43
Kairouan 5/43 11/43
Djedeida 11/43 - 12/43
Cerignola 12/43 - 1/44
Tortorella 1/44 - 10/44
Re-equipped with
Liberators

Points of Interest
No.37 Squadron was one of the six squadrons operational on the Wellington when war was declared and took part in the disastrous Battle of Heligoland Bight in December 1939.

Above: The burnt-out remains of Wellington Mkla P2515 LF-H being inspected by German troops. This aircraft had been hit by flak during a 'Nickel' raid on the night of 23rd-24th March 1940, crashing in flames in a wooded area of the Eifel mountains in Western Germany. Sadly, the second pilot, Sgt Wilson, died in the crash and the pilot, F/O Templeman, died from dreadful burns a few days later – the then P/O Paul Templeman had been 2nd pilot in 'Cheese' Lemon's aircraft during the Battle of Heligoland Bight. The remaining crew escaped to become POWs.

Below: This classic, but almost certainly posed, photograph portrays a hive of activity as ground-crew prepare Mklc T2508 for another operation in the Middle East. This aircraft was at one time the regular mount of F/O 'Cheese' Lemon, the 37 Squadron stalwart who had piloted the only aircraft from the squadron to return from the disastrous Battle of Heligoland Bight, and whose personal motif, a winged lemon, is depicted on the aircraft's nose. By then a Squadron Leader on No.12 Squadron, 'Cheese' Lemon was eventuality shot down by a night-fighter on his way to Duisburg on the night of 25-26th July 1942, becoming a POW.

The Battle of Heligoland Bight

Bomber Command entered the war with the firm belief that a formation of Wellingtons was perfectly capable of defending itself against fighter attack. Early daylight raids against capital ships off the German coast did little to dissuade Bomber Command of this idea, with flak being blamed for the loss of five aircraft from a formation of 12 Wellingtons from 99 Squadron on the 14th December 1939.

Four days later, on Monday 18th December 1939, Bomber Command again put its theory to the test. Led by Wg Cdr Kellett, a formation of 24 Wellingtons drawn from Nos. 9, 37 and 149 Squadrons set out on a shipping search off Wilhelmshaven. As the bombers crossed the North Sea, the cloud cover evaporated leaving unlimited visibility in a bright, crystal clear sky. Two of the bombers left the formation at this time, one with engine trouble and the other, with a remarkable lack of imagination, following the first back to base. The depleted formation pressed on, sighting the island of Sylt at about 12: 30pm. Lowering the 'dustbin' turrets in anticipation of fighter attack, and slowing still further as a result, the formation turned south and proceeded to parade itself down the coast of Schleswig-Holstein heading for Wilhelmshaven.

The first fighters appeared as the formation passed the tiny island of Heligoland but, just as the Me109s of JG77 began their first attacks, the onshore flak batteries opened up. The fighters broke off to one side to wait their turn, watching with incredulity as the Wellingtons, now with bomb doors open, sailed over one battleship and a cruiser lying at anchor off Bau Haven without dropping a single bomb. It was but a temporary reprieve and, as the Wellingtons emerged unscathed from the flak barrage, the carnage began.

The flak barrage had caused the formation to lose cohesion and Wellingtons were now spread dangerously all over the sky. The Me109s, now joined by the Me110s of ZG26, carried out a series of slashing attacks on the lumbering Wellingtons. One by one the Wellingtons fell towards the sea 10,000ft below, flames streaking back from ruptured fuel tanks and the fabric ripped to shreds. Some pilots dropped to sea level in a desperate attempt to evade the pursuing Messerschmitts. Even this desperate measure was to no avail, although at least one Me109 misjudged its attack and cartwheeled into the sea. But it was hardly a fair fight, and 12 of the 22 remaining Wellingtons were shot down or forced to ditch due to loss of fuel. The Battle of Heligoland Bight finally and brutally dispelled the myth that an unescorted formation of Wellingtons could survive in daylight in German skies.

All of the Wellington squadrons taking part in the raid suffered losses, but it was No.37 Squadron that faired worst of all. Bringing up the rear of the formation, No.37 Squadron lost five of the six Wellingtons dispatched from Feltwell that morning. It would almost certainly have lost all six, had not 'Cheese' Lemon's aircraft left the formation in spectacular fashion over Wilhelmshaven, when flaps were mistakenly selected instead of bomb doors, causing the Wellington stall and fall away. One of the Wellingtons lost, N2936 J-Jug, was piloted by Sgt Herbert Ruse. Ruse had taken his aircraft down to sea level and was heading westwards over the Schillig Roads when it was intercepted by the Me110 of Helmut Lent, later a night-fighter 'experten'. With both engines on fire and two crew members dead, Ruse crash-landed his Wellington on the sand dunes on the island of Borkum.

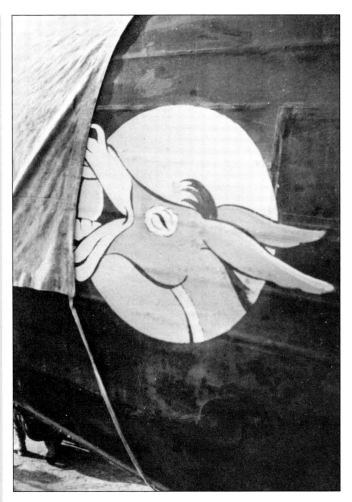

Like many squadrons at this time, 37 Squadron developed a penchant for nose art on its Wellingtons. This donkey adorned X9684 Y-Yorker, although the identity of 'Der Oberhund II' is not known.

Wimpeys in the Desert

Wellington Ic T2748 'K' which had flown with OTUs before being delivered to 37 Squadron.

Wellington Ic T2875 in May 1941. She was lost shortly afterwards on 24th May when she ran out of fuel returning from Maleme and ditched into the Mediterranean.

Wellington Ic Z8787 of 37 Squadron at LG60 in December 1941 without squadron codes. She was taken over by 70 Squadron and lost over Tobruk on 14th September 1942.

LF-K a MkIc at Ma'aten Bagush in 1941.

Above: 'Pinocchio' photographed at Marham in 1940.

38
SQUADRON
Bomber Command
Nov 38 to Nov 40

Code Letters
NH
HD

Middle East
Nov 40 to July 45

Operational bases:
Marham 11/38 - 11/40
Ismailia 11/40 - 12/40
Fayid 12/40
Shallufa 12/40 - 2/43
Berka III 2/43 - 11/44
Kalamaki 11/44 - 12/44
Grottaglie 12/44 - 1/45
Foggia 1/45 - 4/45
Falconara 4/45 - 7/45
Luqa 7/45
Re-equipped with
Warwicks

Points of interest

The squadron was the only one to operate the Wellington throughout the war, starting with MkI in November 1938 and finally relinquishing its GR MkXIVs in December 1946.

Once in the Middle East, 38 Squadron operated the Wellington in both the standard bomber and torpedo bomber role. This is F/Lt Vare RNZAF and crew at Luqa on Malta in 1941, with Wellington Ic Z8736. This aircraft was missing from a raid on Derna on the 27th November 1941.

This posed publicity photo was taken at Malta in 1942. 38 Squadron was instrumental in trialling the Wellington in the torpedo bomber role and carried out the first successful torpedo sorties by Wellington aircraft. The ability to carry two torpedoes and a longer range than the Bristol Beaufort made the Wellington very effective in the torpedo bomber role when operated from Malta. Some of the modifications made to Wellingtons for the torpedo bomber role are evident in this photograph, including the removal of the nose turret, the drift sight in front of the cockpit and the modified bomb-bay doors.

Wellington MkIc Z9028 'Boozee Boze' which was lost on 27th June 1942. Note the toned down fuselage roundel the effect of which which is slightly negated by the large nose art!

Background photo: Wellington Ic W5624 HD-A sits in an open field, probably having just arrived in the Middle East.

Wellington MkVIII HX485 at Gambut in late 1942. She went down in the sea on 11th March 1943.

By the end of the war, 38 Squadron was flying Wellington MkXIVs in the anti-submarine role, seen here on training flight north of Ancona, Italy in the immediate post-war period. The aircraft retain the maritime camouflage scheme of the war years, but with Type C roundels on the upper wings and the squadron crest on the nose.

40

SQUADRON

**Bomber Command
Nov 40 to Oct 41**

**Code Letters
BL**

**Middle East
May 42 to Feb 45**

Operational bases:
Wyton 11/40 - 2/41
Alconbury 2/41 - 10/41

Abu Sueir 5/42 - 6/42
Shallufa 6/42 - 8/42
Kabrit 8/42 - 11/42
LG222A 11/42
LG104 11/42
LG237 11/42 - 1/43
Heliopolis 1/43
LG237 1/43 - 2/43
Gardabia 2/43 - 5/43
El Alem 5/43 - 6/43
Hani West 6/43 - 11/43
Oudna 11/43 12/43
Cerignola 12/43
Foggia 12/43 - 2/43
Re-equipped with
Liberators.

In October 1941, 40 Squadron sent a detachment to Malta on what was intended to be a two-month tour of operations to help the beleaguered island, although in the event the squadron stayed until mid-1942. The MkIc did not have the range to reach Malta direct from the UK and therefore the squadron staged through Gibraltar, although not all of the aircraft dispatched reached their destination. X9889, seen here beneath the famous rock in late October 1941, was one of those that did successfully reach Malta, only to be destroyed in an air raid on Luqa by the end of the year.

"Little Joe", a MkX of 40 Squadron at Kabrit in late 1942, on which the nose turret has been replaced by a fairing fitted with a single fixed 0.303 machine gun. This appears to be a local modification, the purpose of which is not entirely clear, although contemporary photographs show a number of similarly modified aircraft in other squadrons in the Middle East theatre. One suggestion is that the fairing prevents dust from entering the fuselage. Alternatively, the fairing may be a weight-saving measure introduced to offset the fall in performance due to the high air temperatures in the theatre. Whatever the reason, the practice was by no means universal, hinting perhaps at a specialised role for these modified aircraft.

Alconbury House, England, and the sad remains of Sgt Sargents' fatal crash on return from Dusseldorf in the early hours of 3rd June 1941. Sargent and all but one of his crew were killed when U-Uncle stalled and crashed when in the circuit to land at Alconbury, probably the result of the one of the Wellington's less attractive traits – a tendency to drop a wing in turns at low speeds, leading to a unrecoverable stall and spin at low altitudes. The sole survivor of the crash was Sgt Hillebrandt, the rear gunner, who escaped with injuries.

Right: November 1942, ALG 104, Daba.
L-R Sgt Cliff Mortimer (Capt), Sgt Reg Thackeray (2nd pilot), Sgt Rowley Beatson (F/AG), Sgt Wally Hammond (R/AG, Sgt Bert Horton (W/Op) and F/Sgt Jeff Reddell (Nav) .

Below Right: 'What the Hell' HX392 the aircraft of Squadron Leader Steel in March 1942.

Below: A later shot of 'What the Hell' (K-King) in October 42, now flown by Squadron Leader Morton, with an increase in its raid tally.

33

57

SQUADRON
**Bomber Command
Nov 40 to Sept 42**

**Code Letters
DX**

Operational bases:
Feltwell 11/40 - 9/42
Re-equipped with
Lancasters

Despite flying the Wellington for nearly 2 years, there are surprisingly few photos of DX coded Wellingtons around. This one shows DX-B presumably at Feltwell.

57 Squadron flew most of the early marks of the Wellington before converting to Lancasters in September 1942. This fine study of a MkIc of 99 Squadron is typical of the aircraft flown by 57 during the early part of that period. This photograph shows to advantage the slight cut back in the fairing directly behind the front turret made to enable the turret to transverse a full 90 degrees, but which only really succeeded in making the inside of the fuselage even draughtier. The cylindrical object on the side of the fuselage behind the front turret is a thermometer.

69
SQUADRON
**Middle East
Aug 42 to Feb 43**

**Code Letters
No Code**

Operational bases:
Luqa 8/42 - 2/43

Northolt 5/44 - 9/44
Various European bases
9/44 - 8/45

Points of interest

69 Squadron was the only Wellington unit to operate with the 2nd Tactical Air Force, and the first to be based in northern Europe. The unit operated specially modified Wellington Mk XIIIs, with the usual ASV radar removed and optimised for night reconnaissance work.

The C/O of 69 Squadron, Wg Cdr Shaw, with his Flight Commanders, Adjutant and Gunnery Leader and one of the unit's Wellington MkXIIIs at Melsbroek in Belgium, October 1944. The sharply defined camouflage demarcation line inboard of the Hercules engine contrasts sharply with the roughly applied and heavily weathered paintwork outboard.

The aftermath of 'Operation Bodenplatte', the last ditch and ill-fated attempt by the Luftwaffe to regain control of the skies over northern Europe early on the morning of New Year's Day, 1945. This is the scene at Melsbroek, Belgium, where 69 Squadron lost eleven of its Wellingtons in the attack by the Me109s of JG27 and the FW190s of JG54.

A 69 Squadron Wellington XIII over England, June 1944. At this time, the unit was engaged in night reconnaissance over Europe, keeping watch on German troop movements and lines of communication. Uniquely for the type, the unit's Wellingtons were painted in the Dark Green over Medium Sea Grey scheme more commonly associated with Beaufighter and Mosquito night-fighters.

Operational bases:
Kabrit 9/40 - 1/42
LG75 1/42 - 2/42
LG104 2/42 - 6/42
LG224 6/42
Abu Sueir 6/42 - 11/42
LG106 11/42
LG140 11/42 - 1/43
Benina 1/43
El Magrum 1/43 - 2/43
Gardabia 2/43 - 5/43
Temmar 5/43 - 11/43
Djedeida 11/43 - 12/43
Cerignola 12/43
Tortorella 12/43 1/45
Re-equipped with
Liberators

The absence of damage to the bomb-bay doors suggests that the major re-design of the lower nose area of this Wellington was caused by enemy action rather than a crash-landing. Nonetheless, the Wellington made it back to base, proving once again just how resilient the basic structure of the aircraft was.

"The Jeep", a Wellington MkIc of 70 Squadron in 1942. Although the squadron was based at Kabrit for much of this period, operations were usually flown from forward landing grounds nearer the main targets of Tobruk, Derna and Benghazi. This photograph illustrates the primitive operating conditions typically found at the forward landing grounds. "The Jeep" was lost over Derna on 11th November 1942. The Jeep is unusual for a MkI in that the front turret has been replaced with a fairing and the front fuselage windows faired over.

Crew members of 75 (NZ) Squadron, probably at Mildenhall in 1940. Wearing the white flying suit is Wg Cdr Kay DFC, the Commanding Officer at this time. The aircraft behind is an early production MkIc, P9292, still sporting the pre-war camouflage scheme in which the upper surface colours extended down the fuselage sides. The early form of fin flash is also retained, although the yellow surround on the fuselage roundel has been reduced in size in an attempt to make it less conspicuous. This aircraft is believed to have crashed into the sea off the Danish coast on the night of 23rd/24th October 1940 on the way back from Berlin.

Atmospheric shot of ground crews busy preparing N-Nuts of 75 (NZ) Squadron for the operation to Berlin on the 9th/10th April 1941. This major raid for the period was extensively covered by the press, keen no doubt to press home the propaganda value of striking back at the 'The Big City'. This well-known photograph was passed for release by the censor on the 11th April 1941, to become one of the classic images of Bomber Command's early war years.

L4367 in formation with L4370 during an August 1939 defence exercise.

P/O Oliver Matheson (front) and crew, with their personalised Wellington. Directly behind P/O Matheson is the Observer in this crew, P/O Eric Fowler DFC.

75 Squadron aircrew walk past one of their Wellingtons for the benefit of the press in 1941.

The Wellington VC

The only Victoria Cross awarded to a Wellington crew member was gazetted to Sgt James Ward of 75 (NZ) Squadron. On the night of 7/8th July 1941, Sgt Ward was 2nd Pilot to Squadron Leader Reuben Widdowson on a raid to Münster. Approaching the Zuider Zee on the homeward leg, the aircraft was attacked from below by an Me110 night-fighter, causing substantial damage to the starboard engine and hydraulic systems, rupturing a fuel line and knocking out the intercom. Fuelled by the broken pipe, the fire rapidly spread to the starboard wing and all attempts to control the fire from within the cockpit failed. With the cockpit filling with smoke and with no intercom, Widdowson ordered the crew to prepare to abandon the aircraft but Ward convinced his captain to let him have one last attempt at extinguishing the fire, only this time from outside the aircraft.

Wearing his chest parachute and tied to the aircraft with a rope, Ward climbed out of the astrodome on top of the fuselage with the intention of sealing the broken pipe with a canopy cover. To climb down the fuselage, Ward kicked holes in the fabric to use the geodetic structure beneath as foot and hand holds. Moving onto the wing, he edged his way towards the starboard engine, helped by the damage to the fabric caused by the night-fighter attack, but all the time in the slipstream of the airscrew. His task was made all the more difficult by his chest parachute, which prevented him from lying flat to the wing surface, causing the airflow to constantly lift him off the wing and taking all his strength just to maintain his position.

When he reached the broken fuel pipe, Ward encountered another problem. He had tucked the cover underneath his parachute but, as soon as he tried to remove it, the slipstream took hold and nearly dragged him off the wing. After several attempts, Ward eventually succeeded in stuffing the cover into the area where the broken fuel pipe was located but, as soon as he took his hand away, the slipstream blew it out again and the cover disappeared past the rear turret into the night sky.

Ward had no choice other than to retrace his steps and climb back into the aircraft. By now desperately tired, Ward was pulled back through the astrodome by the navigator. Against all odds, Ward's amazing feat of courage had been sufficient to reduce the flames and save his aircraft. Sadly, though, James Ward VC was killed only a few weeks after his award was gazetted when, now the captain of his own crew, his Wellington was shot down by flak over Hamburg.

Above: AA-E protected from the harsh winter. The engines have 'tents' erected around them to enable them to be heated.

Right: Close up of the shattered nose of AA-B after a crash landing.

Left: A group photo taken at Feltwell at the height of the Battle of Britain in September 1940. L-R Henderson, Saxelby, Harkness, Humphries, McCrum and Gosden in front of Wellington Mk Ic R3297 'S'. In the first couple of years of the war, RAF bombs were painted yellow as can been seen here. However, as the bombing offensive increased, stockpiles needed to be stored above ground and the directive was issued to paint all bombs and mines in dark green camouflage.

The presence of the cameraman is clearly a source of amusement for aircrews leaving a pre-ops briefing at Feltwell early in 1941, and may also explain the range of attire amongst the crews. At front left, wearing the greatcoat, is P/O Eric Fowler with, to his right, P/O Barnett. Both were Observers with 75 (NZ) Squadron and both received awards for gallantry at about this time.

93
SQUADRON
**Fighter Command
March 41 to July 41**

**Code Letters
HN**

Operational bases:
Middle Wallop
3/41 - 7/41

Points of interest

93 Squadron was the sole unit in Fighter Command to use the Wellington. The squadron evolved from No.420 ('Pandora') Flight, which itself had been formed at Christchurch in September 1940 for the purpose of testing the 'Pandora' aerial mine, equipped with Handley Page Harrows. The unit was raised to squadron status in December 1940, receiving the first Wellingtons for handling trials that same month. By now renumbered No.93 Squadron, the unit was eventually equipped with two flights of Havocs and a single flight of Wellington Ics, the latter commanded by F/Lt H.G.Goddard. Between March and July 1941, the Wellingtons were engaged in trials of the 'Pandora' aerial mine, in which a curtain of mines suspended by parachutes was intended to be placed in the way of incoming enemy aircraft. The increased effectiveness of AI equipped night-fighters meant that the 'Pandora' mines were never used operationally, and the unit was disbanded in July 1941. The squadron was re-formed in July 1942 on Spitfires and took part in the 'Torch' landings in North Africa.

93 Squadron used the Wellington MkIc for the aerial mining trials. This variant was powered by the 1,050 hp Bristol Pegasus XVII, an example of which is seen here receiving some attention from engine fitters. Evident in this mass of detail are the single row of cylinders of the Pegasus power plant, the engine mounting ring and the supports for the cowling gills. The prominent engine baffle plate, with its distinctive openings, is a characteristic of the Pegasus equipped MkI variants of the Wellington.

99
SQUADRON
Bomber Command
Oct 39 to Feb 42

Code Letters
VF
LN

India
Jun 42 to Sept 44

Operational bases:
Mildenhall 10/38 - 9/39
Newmarket 9/39 - 3/41
Waterbeach 3/41 - 2/42

Ambala 6/42 - 9/42
Pandeveswar
9/42 - 10/42
Digri 10/42 - 4/43
Chaklala 4/43 - 6/43
Jessore 6/43 - 8/44
Dhubalia 8/44 - 9/44
Re-equipped with
Liberators

It was not only operational flying that could be hazardous. The fabric on the rear of this 99 Squadron Wellington MkIa was blown out in flight on a pre-war training sortie although the pilot, Sgt Atkinson, did manage to nurse the aircraft back to the squadron's base at Mildenhall. The aircraft carries the VF code letters used by 99 Squadron pre-war, and is fitted with the early type of Vickers fixed rear turret. Sadly, the then Flt Lt Atkinson was killed in a raid on Essen in May 1943 when serving with a Halifax Pathfinder squadron.

'Semper in Excreta' is the motto of this Wellington LN-J photographed at Newmarket in January 1941.

A snowy study of of T2501 LN-F with the covers on at Newmarket, winter 1940

Left: L-R J H Parry (W/Op), J R Goodman (pilot), G A Master (2nd pilot), G B Cooper (Nav) and R Wickham (A/G) stand with their Wellington T2888 LN-R, at Newmarket in November 1940.

Bottom: A wonderfully atmospheric photo of a Wellington crew boarding LN-B T2984 at Waterbeach on 9th April 1941.

Inset: The following morning an airman surveys the chopped fin of T2739 that returned in this state after a run-in with a night-fighter over Berlin.

Above: On the night of 4/5th December 1940, 83 aircraft set out in bad weather to attack Dusseldorf and Turin. Few of the aircraft reached their target, with one Blenheim and one Wellington being lost. The Wellington was T2501 LN-F from 99 Squadron, piloted by F/O F H Vivian, seen here being inspected by German personnel. The aircraft had been hit by flak on return from Dusseldorf, making a wheels-down emergency landing near Vitry-en-Artois.

P/O W M Dixon being congratulated on his DFC in May 41 for a low-level raid on Brest the previous month.

Below: When war was declared on Japan, 99 and 215 Squadrons were dispatched to India to provide a strategic bombing force in that theatre. Carrying that well known phrase of the period, together with other less repeatable advice to the enemy, "Illegitimo non Carborundum" is seen here at Digri, India late in 1942.

Sqn Ldr Jones and Sgt Dichiel having a last minute conference over the planned route before take-off at Digri, 1942. The absence of any electronic aids and featureless terrain made accurate navigation at night difficult for the Wellington crews. The squadron had been bestowed the additional title of "Madras Presidency" following service in India after WWI, hence the name on the nose of this aircraft.

99 Squadron Wellington on its belly at Jessore, India in February 1944.
The undamaged blades of the port motor point to the cause of the crash-landing being a failure of that engine, whereas the bent prop blades on the starboard motor show that this engine was still running at the point of impact.

Nice air to air of two Wellingtons over the Indian landscape This photograph clearly shows the featureless terrain in this theatre that made navigation at night such a problem for the crews.

101

SQUADRON
Bomber Command
Apr 41 to Oct 42

Code Letters
SR

Operational bases:
West Raynham 4/41 - 7/41
Oakington 7/41 - 2/42
Bourn 2/42 - 8/42
Stradishall 8/42 - 9/42
Holme-on-Spalding Moor
9/42 - 10/42
Re-equipped with
Lancasters

Above: Having run out of fuel on the way back from Hamburg on the night of 30th November/ 1st December 1941, R3295 SR-P of 101 Squadron crash-landed on the tidal flats off Schiermonnikoog, an island in the West Frisian chain. The entire all-sergeant crew were made POWs.

101 Squadron shared the facilities at Oakington with 7 Squadron's Stirlings, the first of the RAF's four-engined 'heavies'. In this photo, an SR coded 101 Sqn Wimpey can be seen tucked away behind the towering bulk of one of the new Stirlings.

With engines already warmed up by the ground crews, a Wellington MkIc is ready for the night's work as the crew arrives. The MkIc was the most capable and most produced of the Pegasus-engined variants of the Wellington, although inferior in performance to the Merlin-engined MkII. The majority of the Wellington units in Bomber Command, including 101 Squadron, were equipped with the MkIc during the early war years.

103

SQUADRON

Bomber Command
Oct 40 to July 42

Code Letters
PM

Operational bases:
Newton 10/40 - 7/41
Elsham Wolds
7/41 - 7/42
Re-equipped with
Halifaxes

Points of interest

103 Squadron was one of very few Bomber Command squadrons to operate four different types of aircraft between 1939 and 1945 flying, in sequence, the Fairey Battle, Vickers Wellington, Handley Page Halifax and Avro Lancaster.

A bad night for Bomber Command

The night of 20th/21st September 1941 was a bad one for Bomber Command, and for 103 Squadron in particular. On this night, Bomber Command dispatched 108 aircraft to attack Berlin and Frankfurt. The mixed force of Hampdens, Whitleys and Wellingtons began leaving their bases in Eastern England from 17:00 onwards, only to be recalled almost immediately due to worsening weather. The problem was fog and amongst the airfields worst affected was Elsham Wolds, home to 103 Squadron. P/O Wallis in L7886 circled the area repeatedly calling for help but eventually, with fuel exhausted, the decision was taken to abandon the aircraft shortly after 4am. All the crew parachuted safely, the empty aircraft crashing at Holton –le – Moor, 4 miles north of Market Rasen (seen here). A second aircraft from the squadron crashed attempting an emergency landing, with five crew killed, and two aircraft from the squadron were lost over enemy territory having failed to heed the recall.

Of the 83 aircraft operating that night, 20 were lost to all causes. Of these, at least ten crashed or were abandoned as a result of poor visibility at base: two crashed due to engine failure: one crashed following collision with a barrage balloon off Spurn Head: and four crashed in England due to unspecified causes. Only three aircraft were lost due to enemy action.

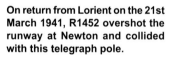

On return from Lorient on the 21st March 1941, R1452 overshot the runway at Newton and collided with this telegraph pole.

Cartoon characters of the period were popular choices when it came to nose art. This is Captain A.R.P. Reilly-Ffoull, squire of "Arntwee Hall" in the popular Daily Mirror cartoon Just Jane. This piece of contemporary nose art adorned Wellington MkIc R1452, PM-G of 103 Squadron.

W5461 EP-R which went missing on the night of 12th August 1941 over Berlin.

104
SQUADRON
Bomber Command
Apr 41 to Feb 42

Code Letters
EP

Middle East
Apr 42 to Feb 45

Operational bases:
Driffield 4/41 - 1/42

Kabrit 1/42 - 5/42
LG106 5/42 - 6/42
Kabrit 6/42 - 11/42
LG224 11/42
LG104 11/42
LG237 11/42 - 2/43
Soluch 2/43
Gardabia 2/43 - 5/43
Cheria 5/43 - 6/43
Hani West 6/43 - 11/43
Oudna 11/43 - 12/43
Cherignola 3 12/43
Foggia 12/43 - 2/45
Re-equipped with
Liberators

Wellington MkII Z8345 crashed on approach to LG121 on the 4th June 1942. At this time, 104 Squadron was engaged in a flurry of operations to cover the retreating 8th Army. Losses were serious, to the extent that tour-expired crews already embarked upon ships for the journey home were recalled for further operations.

A bomb explodes near an EP coded Wellington on Malta.

Top: "Flak-Happy Harry" at dispersal at Foggia, February 1945.

Above: Sgt Doug Skinner in the cockpit of "Flak-Happy Harry".

Right: The crew of "Flak-Happy Harry" on the day after completing their tour of operations, Foggia, 25th February 1945. From left to right: Sgt Wilf Eardley (Nav); Sgt Charlie "Ice-Cool" Williams (R/AG); F/Sgt Jack Gray (Wop); Sgt Doug Skinner (pilot); Sgt Jim Sterrett (B/A).

Above Right: 104 Sqn in action, Trieste harbour under attack from 14,000ft on 17th February 1945.

108
SQUADRON
Middle East
Aug 41 to Nov 42

Code Letters
No Code

Operational bases:
Kabrit 8/41 - 9/41
Fayid 9/41 - 11/42
Re-equipped with
Liberators

Close up of a handily painted nose turret of a 'B' Flight Wellington at Fayid, 1942

'V' Victory gets a scrub down ready for a 'B' Flight photo (see next page).

In sharp contrast to the formality of the squadron photograph, some of the leading characters in the squadron are depicted in a series of sketches by an unknown artist. Could Operational "Jock" "Aye" be standing front row, third from left in the squadron photograph?

The formal 108 Squadron group photograph in front of 'V' a Wellington MkIc, possibly at Fayid, Egypt, late 1941.

Bombing-up Middle East style, The problem of sand getting into engines, guns and other vital equipment was a constant headache and significantly reduced operational efficiency. The front turret of "Pluto" has been faired over to prevent sand from entering the fuselage.

109
SQUADRON
Wireless Development
Dec 40 to Dec 42

Code Letters
HS

Operational bases:
Boscombe Down 12/40 - 1/42
Tempsford 1/42 - 4/42
Stradishall 4/42 - 7/42
Wyton 7/42 - 12/42
Re-equipped with Mosquitos

Points of interest
No.109 Squadron was reformed at Boscombe Down in December 1940 when the Wireless Intelligence Development Unit (WIDU) was raised to full squadron status. The role of the squadron was to research radar aids and radio countermeasures. The squadron was later responsible for the development and introduction of the Oboe bombing aid.

Night-Fighter Bait

By October 1942, British scientists suspected that the Luftwaffe had developed airborne interception radar. The unenviable task of confirming this suspicion fell to 1474 Flight, formed from A Flight of 109 Squadron.

Shortly after 2am on the 3rd December 1942, Sgt Paulton RCAF took from Gransden Lodge in Wellington Ic DV819 to accompany the main force attack on Frankfurt. The plan was for the Wellington to act as bait, in the hope that the frequencies used by the German radar would be picked up by the special equipment on board. The plan worked. At 4:30am, when the aircraft was just to the west of Mainz, P/O Jordan, the special radio operator, began to pick up faint signals on the expected frequency. These signals rapidly increased in intensity, and soon completely swamped the receiver. P/O Jordan just had time to send the coded message confirming the existence of airborne radar and to warn the crew before the aircraft was raked with cannon fire. The pilot threw the aircraft into violent evasive manoeuvres, but the Wellington was severely damaged and four of the crew were injured.

Eventually, the night-fighter vanished and the crew began the long journey home. The aircraft was in a desperate state. One throttle unit had been shot away, the other jammed, and both air speed indicators registered zero. The engines were faltering, both turrets were useless, the hydraulics shot to pieces and the starboard aileron didn't work. The crippled aircraft finally crossed the French coast just before seven in the morning, but was too damaged to attempt a crash-landing. Sgt Paulton therefore ditched the aircraft 200 yards off Walmer beach, south of Deal, at 08;24.

This act of bravery did not go unrewarded. The pilot received the Distinguished Flying Cross, the special radio operator the Distinguished Service Order. The wireless operator, F/Sgt Bigoray, who had sent the vital message despite being seriously injured, received the Distinguished Flying Medal.

Moreover, now that the precise frequencies were known, measures could be put in place to counter the threat posed by radar-equipped night-fighters. One of those measures was known as "Monica", an active radar device to warn bomber crews of approaching fighter aircraft.

115

SQUADRON
Bomber Command
Mar 39 to Mar 43

Code Letters
BK
KO

Operational bases:
Marham 3/39 - 9/42
Mildenhall 9/42 - 11/42
East Wretham
11/42 - 3/43
Re-equipped with
Lancasters

Points of interest

Flew the most raids with the Wellington of any squadron in Bomber Command (332 bombing, 54 mine laying, 4 leaflet).

Flew the most sorties with the Wellington of any squadron in Bomber Command (3075).

Suffered the most losses of any Wellington squadron in Bomber Commend (98) (3.2% of sorties flown).

Carried out the first tests with the 'Gee' navigational aid, August 1941.

An all-sergeant crew of 115 Squadron in front of Wellington Ic R1501 'X' at Marham, March 1941. This aircraft was written off in spectacular style on take-off for Cologne on the night of 26-27th June 1941 when the pilot, Sgt Skillen, retracted the undercarriage prematurely. The fully-laden aircraft sank back down onto the runway and skidded along on its belly, before finally crashing through the boundary fence and coming to rest. Fortunately, there were no injuries.

June 1941 had already been an eventful month for 115 Squadron. Two days prior to Sgt Skillens' abortive take-off, the early-morning calm of a Suffolk village had been shattered by the unexpected arrival of Wellington T2963. The aircraft was returning from Kiel with the pilot, P/O Sharpe, attempting a blind approach with the aid of the Lorenz beam. Just before 05:00, now short of fuel and with the Lorenz equipment malfunctioning, an emergency landing was made in a field adjoining the village of Debach. The Wellington overran the field and careered into houses on the Moat House estate, demolishing one house and severely damaging two others. Two of the crew were seriously injured, with Sgt Tingley succumbing to his injuries the following day. Miraculously, the six occupants of the houses sustained only minor injuries.

L4221 with 115 Squadron's pre-war BK codes in 1939.

German personnel inspect the belly landed hulk of KO-P X9873 on 1st November 1941. She was shot down by Ofw Paul Gildner (4/NJG1) over the island of Schiermonnikoog, Holland.

Another crash landed Wellington R1379 KO-B which became Leutnant Eckart-Wilhelm von Bonin's first night-fighter victory (II/NJG1) on 11th May 1941 at Tonning, Germany. Exactly 50 years later 3 survivors of the crash met von Bonin.

Low viewpoint of a parked Wellington MkIII KO-P X3662. The camouflage demarcation above the wings is unusual.

142
SQUADRON
Bomber Command
Nov 40 to Dec 42

Middle East
Dec 42 to Oct 44

Code Letters
QT
Operational bases:
Binbrook 11/40 - 11/41
Waltham 11/41 - 12/42

Blida 12/42 - 5/43
Fontain Chaude 5/43
Kairouan 5/43 - 11/43
Oudna 11/43 - 12/43
Cerignola 3 12/43 - 2/44
Amendola 2/44 - 7/44
Regina 7/44 - 10/44
Disbanded

Winter scene at Binbrook, 12th December 1940. The squadron had only recently converted from the Fairey Battle and was in the process of working-up with its new Wellington MkIIs at the time. The squadron operated the MkII for only a short period before converting to the Pratt & Whitney engined MkIV in October 1941.

Flt Lt Peter Dobson with air and ground crews gather in front of MkII W5368 at Binbrook in 1941.

MkII W5359 struck off charge in Egypt 6th November 1942.

In December 1942, the squadron moved to the Middle East in support of Allied operations in Tunisia. One of the regular targets was the docks at Bizerta, seen here from 10,000ft in a photograph taken by a 142 Squadron Wellington on the 4th March 1943.

Above: HZ188 QT-D undergoing repairs at Blida following a belly landing.

Below: 142 Squadron Wellingtons HF694 'N' and DF702 'J' at Blida in early 1943. Both aircraft are fitted with a machine gun in the beam window next to the roundel.

148
SQUADRON
Bomber Command
Mar 39 to May 40

Code Letters
BS

Middle East
Dec 40 to Dec 42

Operational bases:
Stradishall 3/39 - 9/39
Harwell 9/39 - 4/40
Stradishall 4/40 - 5/40

Luqa 12/40 - 3/41
Kabrit 3/41 - 5/42
LG106 5/42 - 6/42
Kabrit 6/42 - 8/42
LG237 8/42 - 11/42
LG106 11/42
LG09 11/42 - 12/42
Disbanded

Above: In April 1940, 148 Squadron moved to the Middle East and a year later converted to the more powerful MkII. A pair of the unit's Wellington MkIIs are seen here over the Nile Delta. The extensive weathering on the lead aircraft illustrates to advantage the construction of the Wellington, with the extensive removal of paint from the metal leading edge contrasting with the faded fabric of the fuselage.

Top left: L4304 is an early production MkI, seen here with 148 Squadron in the winter of 1938/39. The aircraft carries the pre-war camouflage scheme, with the disruptive dark green/dark earth pattern extending down the fuselage sides. The absence of a fin flash and the underwing serial numbers are typical of the period, although the stacked call-sign letters in front of the roundel are unusual.

149
SQUADRON
**Bomber Command
Jan 39 to Dec 41**

**Code Letters
OJ**

Operational bases:
Mildenhall 1/39 - 12/41
Re-equipped with
Stirlings

This well known but nonetheless atmospheric shot depicts crews of 149 Squadron walking to their aircraft at Mildenhall, sometime in 1941. The crew member at the left has clearly forgotten something of vital importance, or perhaps wants to avoid the gentleman in the white overalls striding purposefully towards the camera.

"The Ozard of Whiz", the unofficial crest of 149 Squadron. This example adorns "Maximum Effort", which had already completed 14 sorties with the unit by the time this photograph was taken in 1941.

"F for Freddie"

Released in July 1941, Target for Tonight was directed by Harry Watts and was one of the most popular films produced during the war – it is estimated that over 50 million people saw the film in cinemas in Britain and America. The film tells the story of a raid an oil depot at Freihausen by a Wellington squadron based at "RAF Millerton", and follows "Squadron Leader Dixon" and the crew of 'F for Freddie' as they took part in the raid. No actors were involved in making the film, all of the parts being played by the actual RAF personnel involved. The 'in-flight' footage was shot, partly on actual operations and partly using a war-weary Wellington on the airfield.

In reality, the film was shot during March and April 1941 at RAF Mildenhall, home of No.149 Squadron, and 'F for Freddie' is a Wellington Mk1c of that unit. The part of "Squadron Leader Dixon" was played by (then) Squadron Leader Percy Charles Pickard, later Group Captain Pickard DSO DFC of Amiens Prison raid fame, who had been detached to the Crown Film Unit specifically to make the film. Although perhaps best known for leading the low-level attack on the prison, during which he lost his life, "Pick" Pickard had a remarkable career. In the course of over 100 bombing and SOE sorties, Pickard twice brought badly-damaged aircraft back on one engine; ditched in the North Sea once, spending 14 hours in a dinghy; landed a Lockheed Hudson on a waterlogged field in France, at night, and then took-off again in total darkness: and led the Whitley squadron that dropped the parachutists to recover the German Wurzburg radar at Bruneval.

Right: Wellington MkIc L7812 OJ-R. The black fuselage sides have been painted in service hence the unique interpretation, note the serial left on its original green background.

Below: On the night of 10th/11th May 1941, Bomber Command dispatched 119 aircraft to Hamburg. The attack was carried out in perfect visibility under a full moon, and a large number of fires were started in the city. These photographs were taken at Mildenhall on the 10th May, and show the Wellingtons of 149 Squadron being prepared for and setting out on the raid. A total of 60 Wellingtons took part in the raid, of which 3 were lost. One of those belonged to 149 Squadron, Sgt Keymer and crew being lost without trace.

150

SQUADRON

Bomber Command
Oct 40 to Dec 42

Code Letters
JN

Middle East
Dec 42 to Oct 44

Operational bases:
Newton 10/40 - 7/41
Snaith 7/41 - 10/42
Kirmington 10/42 - 12/42

Blida 12/42 - 5/43
Fontaine Chaude 5/43
Oudna 2 11/43 - 12/43
Cerignola 3 12/43 - 2/44
Amendola 2/44 - 7/44
Regina 7/44 - 10/44
Disbanded

Top Right: Sporting one of the most extravagant pieces of nose art ever seen on a Wellington, "Madame 'X'" of 150 Squadron is seen at St.Valentin, Italy, on the 20th August 1944. W/O Walker (centre) and crew are just about to embark on the final operation of their tour.

Right: In early 1943, No.150 Squadron formed part of the North West African Strategic Air Force, commanded by General "Jimmy" Doolittle of the Tokyo Raid fame. Trained in the doctrine of precision bombing in daylight and not being the type of commander content to sit behind a desk, Doolittle wanted to see for himself the technique of bombing by night. On the night of 22nd February 1943, General Doolittle flew in this aircraft as part F/O Roberts' crew on a raid to Bizerta. The cartoon character is again J P Reilly Foul, accompanied this time by a lucky horseshoe below the front turret.

Below: LN323 of 150 Squadron takes off from Kairouan West, Tunisia on 8th September 1943.

Below: A DWI Wellington of 162 Squadron warms up its engines at an airfield in the Suez Canal Zone. Despite its ungainly appearance, the 48ft diameter coil had remarkably little effect on the flying characteristics of the Wellington.

Inset: The unique plan view of a DWI Wellington.

156 SQUADRON
Bomber Command
Feb 42 to Jan 43

Code Letters
GT

Operational bases:
Alconbury 2/42 - 8/42
Warboys 8/42 - 1/43
Re-equipped with
Lancasters

158 SQUADRON
Bomber Command
Feb 42 to Jun 42

Code Letters
NP

Operational bases:
Driffield 2/42 - 6/42
East Moor 6/42
Re-equipped with
Halifaxes

162 SQUADRON
Middle East
Jan 42 to Sept 44

Code Letters
No Code

Operational bases:
Kabrit 1/42
Shallufa 1/42 - 4/42
Bilbeis 4/42 - 4/43
Benina 4/43 - 8/43
LG91 8/43 - 4/44
Idku 4/44 - 9/44
Disbanded

Points of interest

Formed from a detachment of No.109 Squadron at Kabrit, Egypt in January 1942, the unit was known for several weeks as the Signals Squadron before being formally numbered 162 Squadron. The squadron was mainly involved in radio calibration and radio counter measures work using Wellingtons and Bristol Blenheims. In March 1944, the squadron took over the DWI Wellingtons of 1GRU, using them in the minesweeping role until July of that year.

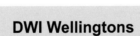

DWI Wellingtons

The Wellington DWI was a response to the serious threat posed by German magnetic sea mines. The sea mines were designed to detonate as a result of an increase in the magnetic field caused by a passing ship. Examination of an intact mine recovered from mud flats off Shoeburyness revealed that detonation would also occur if a magnetic field of sufficient strength could be generated from an aircraft flying overhead.

Vickers was approached to modify the Wellington to carry a 51ft diameter balsa hoop containing an aluminium coil, through which a 35kw generator carried aboard the aircraft created an electro-magnetic field. To save weight, nose and tail turrets were replaced by streamlined fairings and all unnecessary equipment was removed. The converted aircraft were known as Wellington DWI (Directional Wireless Installation) MkIs, although this was of course a deliberate misnomer intended to conceal the true purpose of the equipment.

Initial trials showed promise, although some experimentation with speed and height was required to avoid damage to the DWI aircraft from detonating mines. A total of fifteen MkIa and MkIc aircraft were converted, later examples being equipped with a more powerful 95kw generator and a smaller diameter (48ft) hoop. These aircraft were known as Wellington DWI MkIIs, and were a significant improvement over the DWI MkI. Both versions were operated from Manston by a specially formed unit, No. 1 General Reconnaissance Unit (1GRU), this being another deliberate misnomer. The first mine was detonated on the 8th January 1940 and thereafter steady, if not spectacular, results were obtained. In May 1940, 1GRU moved to the Middle East to cover the Suez Canal.

166 SQUADRON
Bomber Command
Jan 43 to Sept 43

Code Letters
AS

Operational bases:
Kirmington 1/43 - 9/43
Re-equipped with
Lancasters

172
SQUADRON
**Coastal Command
Apr 42 to June 45**

**Code Letters
WN
OG
1**

Operational bases:
Chivenor 4/42 - 9/44
Limavady 9/44 - 6/45
Disbanded

Points of interest

Formed at Chivenor from
1417 (Leigh Light) Flight on
the 4th April 1942.

The intricacies of flying clothing are explained to Mr W J Jordan, High Commissioner for New Zealand, on a visit to 172 Squadron in November 1942. Just visible in the hangar behind is one of the unit's Wellington GRVIIIs which, despite its maritime role, carries the night bomber scheme typical of early production examples.

Reflecting their nocturnal anti-submarine origins, the squadron motto was "Insidiantibus insidamur" (We ambush the ambusher). From August 1943, the squadron operated the ASV and Leigh Light equipped Wellington MkXIV, several examples of which await the next patrol at Chivenor in 1944.

The '1' code on this aircraft stems from the period when RAF Coastal Command stopped using squadron codes. To differentiate between squadrons on the same base, a simple numbering system was introduced, with number 1 usually going to the lowest numbered squadron, and then 2 and 3 being applied in a similar fashion.

179
SQUADRON
Coastal Command
Nov 42 to 11/44

Code Letters
OZ

Operational bases:

Skitten 9/42 - 11/42
Gibraltar 11/42 - 4/44
Predannack 4/44 - 9/44
Chivenor 9/44
Benbecula 9/44 - 10/44
Chivenor 10/44 - 11/44
St Eval 11/44
Re-equipped with
Warwicks

Points of interest

Formed at Skitten from a detachment of 172 Squadron on the 1st September 1942. Moved to Gibraltar in November 1942 for anti-submarine patrols in the Med. Squadron motto was similar in style to its parent unit; "Delenterm deleo" (I destroy the destroyer).

By then equipped with the GRXIV, 179 Squadron returned to the UK in April 1944 tasked with closing the Channel to U-boats in preparation for the Normandy landings. The Wellington GRXIV was fitted with metal plates under part of the wing outside of the engine nacelle, thereby enabling it to carry up to eight rockets. Combined with ASV MkIII and the Leigh Light, rocket equipped GRXIVs were certainly capable of living up to the squadron's motto "Delenterm deleo" (I destroy the destroyer).

In November 1944, 179 Squadron converted to the Vickers Warwick. Designed in parallel with the Wellington, the Warwick was originally intended to be a heavy bomber but delays in development meant that the aircraft would have been obsolescent in that role even before entering service. The Warwick did however see extensive use in the transport and air-sea rescue roles.

RCM and ELINT Wellingtons

The Wellington had a long association with Radio Counter Measures (RCM) and electronic intelligence (ELINT) work. As early as 1940, Wellingtons were employed by the Wireless Intelligence Development Unit (WIDU) in the search for the German blind bombing aids Knickebein and Y Gerät, and were later used to confirm the existence of German airborne interception radar (see 109 Squadron). In the Middle East, the ELINT role was performed by the Wellingtons of 162 squadron, which also used Wellingtons equipped with 'Jostle' transmitters to block communications between German armoured vehicles.

The Wellington is, however, more commonly known for its counter-measures work in support of the bomber offensive. As part of 100 Group, Wellingtons of 192 Squadron deployed a variety of jamming devices in support of Main Force raids as well as conducting 'Big Ben' jamming operations against V2 rockets. The slower Wellingtons could not keep pace with the Lancasters and Halifaxes of the Main Force, and therefore patrolled the western seaboard of Occupied Europe while the squadron's Halifaxes accompanied the bombers. The squadron was also engaged in ELINT work over Holland, Denmark and Germany. The last of the Wellingtons were eventually withdrawn in November 1944, finally bringing to an end the Wellington's service in Bomber Command.

192
SQUADRON
Special Duties
Radio/Radar Trials
Jan 43 to Jan 45

Code Letters
DT

Operational bases:
Gransden Lodge
1/43-1/45

Points of interest
192 Squadron was formed from 1474 Flight in January 1943, itself formed from A Flight of 109 Squadron, and a year later also absorbed 1473 Flight. The unit was unusual in that it had a much larger establishment than a normal bomber squadron and flew a variety of aircraft, including the Wellington, Halifax and Mosquito. The squadron concentrated on RCM/ELINT work throughout its existence, becoming part of 100 Group in December 1943. In November 1944, the unit fully converted to the Halifax.

196
SQUADRON
**Bomber Command
Dec 42 to July 43**

**Code Letters
ZO**

Operational bases:
Leconfield 12/42 - 7/43
Re-equipped with
Stirlings

199
SQUADRON
**Bomber Command
Nov 42 to July 43**

**Code Letters
EX**

Operational bases:
Blyton 11/42 - 2/43
Ingham 2/43 - 6/43
Lakenheath 6/43 - 7/43
Re-equipped with
Stirlings

203
SQUADRON
**Middle East
Nov 43 to Oct 44**

**Code Letters
No Code**

Operational bases:
Santa Cruz
11/43 - 10/44
Re-equipped with
Liberators

214
SQUADRON
**Bomber Command
May 39 to Apr 42**

**Code Letters
UX
BU**

Operational bases:
Feltwell 5/39 - 9/39
Methwold 9/39 - 2/40
Stradishall 2/40 - 1/42
Honington 1/42
Stradishall 1/42 - 4/42
Re-equipped with Stirlings

A 203 Squadron Wellington XIII JA176 / K flown by S/L Scotney 11th November 1943.

Right: Taken at Stradishall in 1941, this posed photograph shows air and ground crews inspecting a flak-damaged Wellington MkIc of 214 Squadron. The long cylindrical object being examined by the group on the left appears to be a long-range fuel tank, whereas the group to the right are inspecting an inner bomb-bay door.

Below: Into the breach once more...... a 214 Squadron Wellington sets out from its home base at Stradishall. The elegant wing shape of the Wellington is evident, in stark contrast to the somewhat dumpy shape of the fuselage.

The fortunes of war are no better illustrated than by the fate of this aircraft, MkIa N2912 of 215 Squadron, seen here at Bassingbourn in mid-1940. A year later, when engaged in night circuit training, this aircraft was shot down directly over Bassingbourn by an intruder piloted by Fw Gieszubel of I/NJG2. Completely out of control, the stricken bomber crashed onto the airfield where, amidst acres of open space, it crashed directly onto another of the unit's aircraft parked at dispersal. The eighteen year old pilot, Sgt Alstrom, and thirty year old Sgt Wilson were both killed although the third crew member, Sgt Nicholls, walked from the wreckage with only minor injuries.

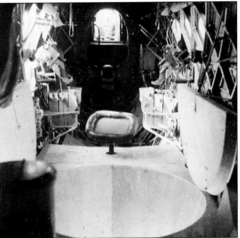

By 1943, 215 Squadron was engaged in dropping parachutists in India. These photographs show the well in the fuselage through which the parachutists exited, originally the position for the 'dustbin' turret on the early Wellington variants, and a training drop of the 10th Gurka Paratroop Battalion near Rawalpindi.

Wellington Ic R1448 HA-L 'Akyem Abuakwa' at Marham in 1941. This aircraft flew 218's final Wellington sortie during Operation Fuller 12th February 1942.

221

SQUADRON

Coastal Command
Nov 40 to Jan 42

Code Letters
DF

Middle East
Jan 42 to Aug 45

Operational bases:
Bircham Newton
11/40 - 5/41
Limavady 5/41 - 9/41
Reykjavik 9/41 - 12/41
Docking 12/41 - 1/42

LG39 1/42 - 2/42
LG87 2/42 - 3/42
LG89 3/42 - 6/42
Shandur 6/42 - 8/42
Shallufa 8/42 - 2/43
Luqa 2/43 - 3/44
Grottaglie 3/44 - 10/44
Kalamaki 10/44 - 4/45
Idku 4/45 - 8/45
Disbanded

Above: A GRVIII HX604 'X' on a rocky dispersal very typical of Malta.

Right: With bomb doors gaping, a 221 Squadron MkXIII makes a practice runner attack on a British destroyer off Malta, December 1943. At this time, the squadron was mostly engaged in anti-submarine patrols, specialising in night torpedo attacks.

Left: A MkVIII with ASV MkII aerials, under wing array and turrets for a day torpedo role.

Below: Wellington MkXIIIs including MF263 'F' of 221 Squadron based at Kalamaki, Greece, parked on Sedes airfield after transporting men and supplies to the Allied forces operating in the Salonika area.

A similar story

Both 232 and 242 Squadrons previously flew Spitfire IXs from Corsica in support of the invasion of southern France. After the invasion, both squadrons withdrew to Naples where 232 was disbanded on 31st October 1944, 242 on the 4th November 1944. Both squadrons reformed on 15th November 1944 at Stoney Cross, equipped with Wellington Mk XVIs for training in the transport role. 232 was re-equipped with Liberators in January 1945, 242 with Stirling MkIVs the following month.

232
SQUADRON
Coastal Command
Dec 44

Code Letters
No Code

Operational bases:
Stoney Cross 12/44
Re-equipped with
Liberators

242
SQUADRON
Coastal Command
Jan 45 to Feb 45

Code Letters
No Code

Operational bases:
Stoney Cross 1/45 - 2/45
Re-equipped with
Stirlings

244
SQUADRON
Middle East
Feb 44 to May 45

Code Letters
No Code

Operational bases:
Sharjah 2/44 - 3/44
Masirah 3/44 - 5/45
Disbanded

A 221 Squadron MkXIII JA416 over Malta in January 1944. 244 Squadron also operated the MkXIII in the anti-submarine role.

R1720 'City of Nottingham' was purchased by the city for £20,000 and donated to the RAF. Built as a MkIc it served with 11, 12 and 14 OTUs before being converted to a MkXVI and joining 242 Squadron. It survived the war and was scrapped in May 1946.

281
SQUADRON
Coastal Command
Air Sea Rescue
Aug 45 to Sept 45

Code Letters
FA

Operational bases:
Ballykelly 8/45 - 9/45
Disbanded

Points of interest

281 Squadron reformed at Thornaby in November 1943, equipped with Warwicks and Sea Otters in the ASR role. The squadron operated a few Wellington MkXIVs from Tiree in September 1945.

281 Squadron mainly flew Warwicks like this one and only had Wellingtons for about a month.

Before 294 Squadron was formed, the area was covered by Sea Rescue Flights. This Wellington MkIc photographed in October 1942, is from one of the Egyptian based Sea Rescue Flights

A poor quality but interesting shot of a 294 Squadron Wellington MkXIII at Idku, March 1945. In addition to the standard ASV aerial fit, this aircraft carries an additional fitting under the front turret, the purpose of which is not known, although it may be related to the Air Sea Rescue role that was the primary task of the squadron.

294
SQUADRON
Middle East
Air Sea Rescue
Oct 43 to June 45

Code Letters
No Code

Operational bases:
LG91 10/43 - 3/44
Idku 3/44 - 6/45
Re-equipped with
Warwicks

300
SQUADRON
Bomber Command
Dec 40 to Apr 44

Code Letters
BH

Operational bases:
Swinderby 12/40 - 7/41
Hemswell 7/41 - 5/42
Ingham 5/42 - 1/43
Hemswell 1/43 - 6/43
Ingham 6/43 - 3/44
Faldingworth 3/44 - 4/44
Re-equipped with
Lancasters

5th September 1942, Flt Lt Marian Wlodarczyk and the crew of Z1407 BH-Z 'Zoska' pose with their aircraft after bringing it back from Bremen with no fabric on the rear fuselage.

The position of the fuselage windows between different marks of Wellington dictated where the squadron codes were placed on the port side. BH-T has the squadron code aft of the roundel whereas BH-W has it forward.

Wellington MkX HF598 BH-E awaits its load of mines.

301

SQUADRON

Bomber Command
Oct 40 to Apr 43

Code Letters
GR

Operational bases:
Swinderby 10/40 - 7/41
Hemswell 7/41 - 4/43
Disbanded

Quite why the pilot of this 301 Squadron machine is wearing an oxygen mask and concentrating firmly on the horizon is a bit of a mystery, because the aircraft is quite clearly stationary. This is another example of transferring the insignia of a Polish Air Force squadron to an RAF aircraft, in this case the 41st Light Bomber Regiment, which flew the PZL 23 "Karas" light bomber in the defence of Poland in September 1939.

Originally captioned "Poles repay Nazis with bombs" and released to the British press in December 1940, this photograph shows bombing-up of a 301 Squadron Wellington at Swinderby. Notwithstanding the chill of a winter's day on an airfield in Lincolnshire, these Polish Air Force personnel seem decidedly inappropriately dressed for the job in hand. The aircraft in the background came to grief in bizarre circumstances when later in the service of 18 OTU at Bramcote. Whilst undergoing an engine change, and with the port engine suspended by a crane, the motor slipped and sparks set fire to a tray containing paraffin. The resultant fire set the aircraft's fabric alight and the bomber was destroyed in the conflagration.

304

SQUADRON
Bomber Command
Nov 40 to May 42

Coastal Command
May 42 to July 45

Code Letters
NZ
2
QD

Operational bases:
Bramcote 11/40 - 13/40
Syerston 12/40 - 7/41
Lindholme 7/41 5/42

Tiree 5/42 - 6/42
Dale 6/42 - 11/42
Talbenny 11/42 - 12/42
Dale 12/42 - 4/43
Docking 4/43 - 6/43
Davidstowe Moor 6/43
- 12/43
Predannack 12/43 - 2/44
Chivenor 2/44 - 9/44
Benbecula 9/44 - 3/45
St Eval 3/45 - 7/45
North Weald 7/45
Re-equipped with
Warwicks

On the 24th April 1942, the Polish Commander-in-Chief, General Sikorsky, visited Lindholme, exactly one year to the day on which 304 Squadron had undertaken its first operational sortie. Centre of attention of the General's entourage is "Sonia", a Wellington MkIc of 304 Squadron, which has evidently made a wheels-up landing with at least one engine still turning. The squadron suffered no operational losses in the days leading up to General Sikorsky's visit, and it is therefore assumed that "Sonia" has suffered a training accident.

Left: NZ-F R3212 was a veteran when this photo was taken having already served with four other units before joining 304.

Below: A view across Lindholme with three 304 Sqn Wellingtons including NZ-Q DV441.

Inset: R1697 with a ventilated fin back at Syerston in 1941.

Two views of 304 Sqn Wellingtons at Dale in early 1943, 'T' is DV597.
Below: Wellington MkX HZ258 'S' of 304 Squadron on patrol.

The crew of HF330 2-N inspect the damage suffered after an attack on a U-Boat in the Bay of Biscay, 5th May 1944. The '2' code indicated that they were the second squadron (after 172) at Chivenor.

Above: Detailed close-up of the cockpit of a 304 Squadron Wellington at Dale. Note the windscreen washer pipes on the nose.

Above and Left: 304 Squadron GRXIVs at Chivenor in 1944. These aircraft carry an extra DF fairing in front of the standard fitting and a radio altimeter aerial just below the cockpit.

Below: 304 Squadron MkXIVs at St Eval in April 1945.

305 SQUADRON

**Bomber Command
Nov 40 to Sept 43**

**Code Letters
SM**

Operational bases:
Bramcote 11/40 - 12/40
Syerston 12/40 - 7/41
Lindholme 7/41 - 7/42
Hemswell 7/42 - 6/43
Ingham 6/43 - 9/43
Swanton Morley 9/43
Re-equipped with
Mitchells

Above Right: A rare air-to-air shot of SM-Z over England on a training flight.

Right: Waiting for inspiration! A MkII awaits its bombs.

Below: 305 Squadron on parade at Lindholme, 25th April 1942. The aircraft in the foreground, MkII W5590, was lost a week later when it ditched in the North Sea returning from Hamburg. The crew were all rescued unhurt 10 hours after setting out from Lindholme, having spent an uncomfortable night in the dinghy. Unusually, this squadron was in the habit of recording sorties above the fin flash.

Above: Another groundcrew who seem in no particular hurry to bomb up this MkII at Lindholme.

Right: ... And another example of the squadron's unusual habit of painting bomb tallies on the tail.

Below: The squadron eventually received Wellington MkXs like this one to replace their older MkIIs.

The ubiquitous tractor being used to tow a 305 Squadron Wellington MkII W5455 SM-L back to the hangar.

311

SQUADRON

Bomber Command
July 40 to April 1942

Coastal Command
April 1942 to May 1943

Code Letters
KX

Operational bases:
Honington 7/40 - 9/40
East Wretham 9/40 - 4/42
Aldergrove 4/42 - 6/42
Talbenny 6/42 5/43
Re-equipped with
Liberators

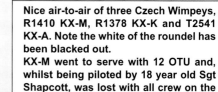

Nice air-to-air of three Czech Wimpeys, R1410 KX-M, R1378 KX-K and T2541 KX-A. Note the white of the roundel has been blacked out.

KX-M went to serve with 12 OTU and, whilst being piloted by 18 year old Sgt Shapcott, was lost with all crew on the last of the Thousand Bomber Raids on the 25th/"26th June 1942.

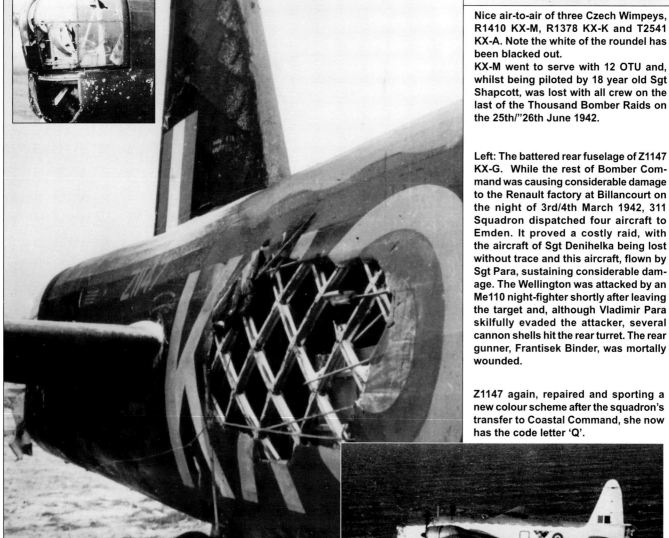

Left: The battered rear fuselage of Z1147 KX-G. While the rest of Bomber Command was causing considerable damage to the Renault factory at Billancourt on the night of 3rd/4th March 1942, 311 Squadron dispatched four aircraft to Emden. It proved a costly raid, with the aircraft of Sgt Denihelka being lost without trace and this aircraft, flown by Sgt Para, sustaining considerable damage. The Wellington was attacked by an Me110 night-fighter shortly after leaving the target and, although Vladimir Para skilfully evaded the attacker, several cannon shells hit the rear turret. The rear gunner, Frantisek Binder, was mortally wounded.

Z1147 again, repaired and sporting a new colour scheme after the squadron's transfer to Coastal Command, she now has the code letter 'Q'.

24th September 1940 - Leidschendam, Germany. German Officers inspect the wreck of L7788 KX-E after it crash landed . This was the squadron's first operational loss.

The battered remains of KX-K R1378 after a crash landing. Despite the extent of the damage it was repaired only to be lost in March 1942.

Port wing ablaze from a ruptured fuel tank, this remarkable photo is believed to show the final seconds of KX-T, T2990. Taken at 02:13 on the morning of 23rd June 1941, the aircraft was attacked on the way back from Bremen by an Me110 night-fighter flown by Oblt. Prinz zur Lippe-Weissenfeld of 4/NJG1. Moments later, the Wellington plunged into the Kosterveloren Polder with only the pilot, Flt Sgt Bufka, escaping to become a POW.

Replenishing the oil tank of 311 Squadron Wellington R1598 in an almost rural setting at East Wretham, Spring 1941. The airman beneath the wing holding the oil line nozzle waits patiently as his colleague, looking less than confident of his footing, inches his way towards the filler cap.

A weak winter sun reflects from the fuselage windows as "Z-Zebra" stands all alone on a snow-covered East Wretham. When it came to markings, 311 Squadron was a law unto itself. Many of the unit's aircraft carried full height code letters with oversize fuselage roundels, the latter of which were often overpainted in service to reduce their conspicuousness.

Left and Below Left: The result of a rapidly moving force meeting an immovable object. Piloted by F/O Josef Stransky, this aircraft developed an uncontrollable swing on take-off from East Wretham on the 19th July 1941, swerved off the runway and collided with a steam roller. The aircraft was a write-off, although happily the crew escaped without serious injury.

Below: By now a Squadron Leader and with a Distinguished Flying Cross to his name, Josef Stransky brought this flak-damaged aircraft back from Bremen on the third of the Thousand Bomber Raids, 26th June 1942. By this time, 311 had been transferred to Coastal Command and Josef Stransky's Wellington was one of 102 aircraft from Coastal Command that, on the express instructions of Winston Churchill, had been allowed to take part in the raid.

Below: 9th April 1941. Close up of the fuselage of P9230 KX-X after being attacked by a Ju88 intruder and crash landing.

A flak damaged R1777 KX-M lies on her belly after returning to East Wretham from a raid on Mannheim, April 1942.

R1161 displays a small identification letter unlike the other KX-X on the page opposite.

Below Right: Another example of the same code letter on different aircraft, KX-F is X9827 and KX-F (Below) is Z1155. The latter was eventually lost on an anti-submarine patrol on 15th July 1942 when Flt Sgt Hugo Dostal and his crew were shot down by a Ju88C-6 of IV/KG40 over the Bay of Biscay.

344

SQUADRON

**N Africa
Nov 43 to Nov 45**

**Code Letters
No Codes**

Operational bases:
Dakar 11/43 - 11/45
Disbanded and became
a French unit

Above: 344 Squadron was formed from a French unit that had been flying anti-submarine patrols in North Africa. After the war it once again came under French control still flying Wellingtons, these French marked aircraft are pictured in 1947.

Right: The sortie tally and generally worn appearance confirm that "Moonshine" of 405 Squadron is a veteran of twenty-three ops over Germany. The 'B' denotes operations to Berlin although, when this photograph was taken on the 3rd April 1942, Bomber Command had not visited "The Big City" for nearly five months.

Below Right: F/Lt Jack Mac-Cormack in the cockpit of "Dummy Run", a 405 Squadron Wellington MkII at Pocklington, 14th August 1941. The usual extensive fuselage side glazing has been replaced with smaller window apertures on this aircraft.

405

SQUADRON

**Bomber Command
May 41 to Apr 42**

**Code Letters
LQ**

Operational bases:
Driffield 5/41 - 6/41
Pocklington 6/41 - 4/42
Re-equipped with
Halifaxes

Points of interest

405 Squadron was the first Canadian squadron to form overseas and the only RCAF Pathfinder squadron.

Below: On the 3rd April 1942, the press descended on Pocklington and 405 "Vancouver" Squadron. This photograph shows P/O W A McKay, appropriately enough a native of Vancouver, at the controls of one of the unit's Wellingtons.

407
SQUADRON
Coastal Command
Jan 43 to June 45

Code Letters
1
2
RR

Operational bases:

Docking 1/43 - 2/43
Skitten 2/43 - 4/43
Chivenor 4/43 - 11/43
S Eval 11/43 - 12/43
Limavady 12/43 - 4/44
Chivenor 4/44 - 8/44
Wick 8/44 11/44
Chivenor 11/44 - 6/45
Disbanded

Wellington MkII W5637 LQ-O photographed at Driffield on 16th July 1941. She was lost 8 days later in a raid on the Gneisenau.

Left: Wellington XIV NB839 2-R at Chivenor in 1944, note the invasion stripes around the rear fuselage.

Below: Wellington XII HP113/G of 407 "Demon" Squadron RCAF over the Taw Estuary, heading for its base at Chivenor. The 'G' suffix to the serial indicates that the aircraft must be kept under armed guard when on the ground probably, in this case, because of the ASV III radar under the nose.

415
SQUADRON
**Coastal Command
Sept 43 to July 44**

**Code Letters
NH**

Operational bases:
Thorney Island
9/43 - 11/43
Bircham Newton
11/43 - 7/44
Re-equipped with
Halifaxes

Above: A Wellington MkXIII of No. 415 Squadron RCAF at Bircham Newton, April 1944. The MkXIII was a development of the MkX bomber specifically for the daylight torpedo bombing role and many, including MF639 here, were delivered in standard Bomber Command camouflage schemes. In addition to the usual aerial array for the ASV II, this aircraft carries two 'T' shaped radio altimeters beneath the rear fuselage to enable accurate height to be maintained during the torpedo run.

419
SQUADRON
**Bomber Command
Jan 42 to Nov 42**

**Code Letters
VR**

Operational bases:
Mildenhall 1/42 - 8/42
Leeming 8/42
Topcliffe 8/42 - 10/42
Croft 10/42 - 11/42
Re-equipped with
Halifaxes

Above: "Moosemen" quite at home in the snow at Mildenhall, 9th February 1942. From left to right: Sqn Ldr F W S Turner; P/O K E Hobson; F/Sgt G P Fowler; F/Sgt C A Robson; F/Sgt N G Arthur; F/Sgt H T Dell. Tragically, after completing his tour with this crew, F/Sgt Dell volunteered for one more sortie with the C/O, Wing Commander "Moose" Fulton, and was killed along with his C/O on the way back from Hamburg on the night of 28/29th July 1942.

Left: Wing Commander John "Moose" Fulton DFC, AFC and his Observer, F/Sgt E S "Red" Alexander, examine their battered aircraft on the morning after the Kiel operation, 29th April 1942. "Moose" Fulton was awarded the Distinguished Service Order for bringing his severely damaged aircraft back to base, with F/Sgt Alexander receiving the Distinguished Flying Medal for his part in the operation.

420
SQUADRON
**Bomber Command
Aug 42 to Dec 43
except Middle East
Jun 43 to Oct 43**

**Code Letters
PT**

Operational bases:
Skipton-on-Swale
8/42 - 10/42
Middleton St George
10/42 - 5/43
Kairouan 6/43 - 9/43
Hani East 9/43 - 10/43
Dalton 11/43 12/43
Tholthorpe 12/43
Re-equipped with
Halifaxes

Squadron Leader Joe McCarthy of 424 Squadron poses with "Terror of the Axis Night Life" at Kairouain, Tunisia, 28th September 1943.

Below: The happy disposition of this 425 Squadron crew, in daytime at least, somehow seems at odds with the name given to their aircraft. Kairouain, 31st August 1943.

Left: Despite the impressive sortie tally, including the DFC ribbon, the bomb-carrying winged turtle and the name are very apt for a Wellington. It is not clear whether the lighter colour bomb symbols represent daylight raids, or whether the store has run out of red paint.

424
SQUADRON
Bomber Command
Oct 42 to Nov 43
except Middle East
May 43 to Oct 43

Code Letters
QB

Operational bases:
Topcliffe 10/42 - 4/43
Leeming 4/43 - 5/43
Dalton 5/43
Kairouan 6/43 - 9/43
Hani East 9/43 - 10/43
Skipton-on-Swale 11/43
Re-equipped with
Halifaxes

Two nice air-to-air shots of Wellington MkIIIs from the same production batch. X3763 KW-E cruising over cloud was shot down over Stuttgart on 14th April 1943.

X3803 KW-H was more fortunate, being passed on to 20 OTU before being scrapped in 1947.

425
SQUADRON
Bomber Command
Aug 42 to Dec 43
except Middle East
May 43 to Sept 43

Code Letters
KW

Operational bases:
Dishforth 8/42 - 5/43
Kairouan 5/43 - 9/43
Dishforth 11/43 -12/43
Tholthorpe 12/43
Re-equipped with
Halifaxes

426 SQUADRON
Bomber Command
Oct 42 to June 43

Code Letters
OW

Operational bases:
Dishforth 10/42 - 6/43
Linton-on-Ouse 6/43
Re-equipped with
Lancasters

427 SQUADRON
Bomber Command
Nov 42 to May 43

Code Letters
ZL

Operational bases:
Croft 11/42 - 5/43
Leeming 5/43
Re-equipped with
Halifaxes

428 SQUADRON
Bomber Command
Nov 42 to June 43

Code Letters
NA

Operational bases:
Dalton 11/42 - 6/43
Middleton St George 6/43
Re-equipped with
Halifaxes

429 SQUADRON
Bomber Command
Nov 42 to Aug 43

Code Letters
AL

Operational bases:
East Moor 11/42 - 8/43
Leeming 8/43
Re-equipped with
Halifaxes

Left: Wellington III BJ668 ZL-X of 427 Squadron at Croft in early 1943.

Below: Wellington X HE429 AL-Q of 429 Squadron which crashed at East Moor returning from Duisburg on 13th May 1943.

Bottom: A line-up of 426 Squadron Wellington MkXs including OW-A at Dishforth early 1943.

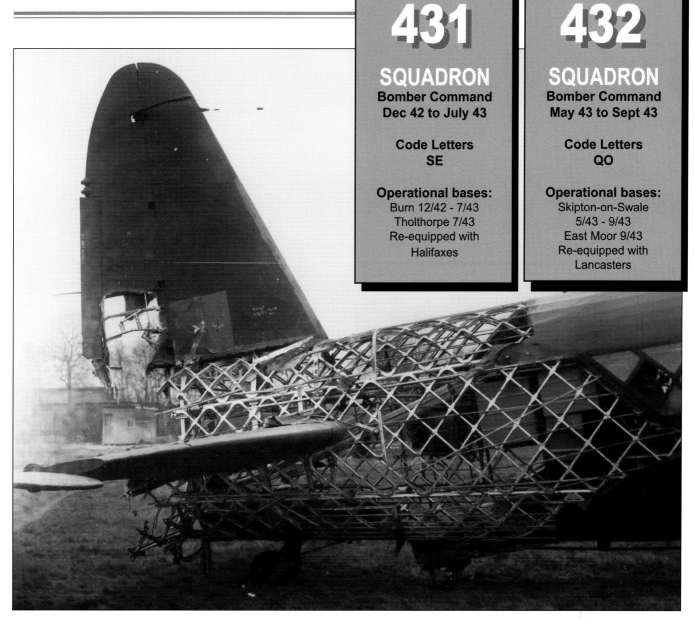

431 SQUADRON
Bomber Command
Dec 42 to July 43

Code Letters
SE

Operational bases:
Burn 12/42 - 7/43
Tholthorpe 7/43
Re-equipped with
Halifaxes

432 SQUADRON
Bomber Command
May 43 to Sept 43

Code Letters
QO

Operational bases:
Skipton-on-Swale
5/43 - 9/43
East Moor 9/43
Re-equipped with
Lancasters

A direct hit from flak completely removed the rear turret and much of the fabric on the rear fuselage of this Wellington X, HE1158 NA-L of 428 Squadron. The aircraft was one of 392 aircraft participating in an ineffectual attack on Duisburg on the night of 8th/9th April 1943, of which 19 were lost. Amongst the losses was P/O Buckham's crew from 428 Squadron, although they all survived to become POW's.

432 Squadron shared their base with 420 Squadron, and it is G-for George of the latter unit that is seen here setting off from Skipton-on-Swale in mid-1943. The fickle hand of fate could play a funny game, and it did not take long for particular call-signs to become either lucky or jinxed in the minds of aircrew. It was about this time, mid-1943, that 432 Squadron experienced one of those peculiar twists of fate that were so common in wartime. In spite of a steady succession of losses since becoming operational in May 1943, "G-George" of 432 Squadron had always come back. That is until late August, when two aircraft with that call-sign failed to return in the space of less than three weeks. Such random swipes of the 'Grim Reaper's' scythe cannot be explained, but nonetheless played a major part in the psyche of aircrew.

458

SQUADRON
(Australian)
Bomber Command
Aug 41 to Mar 42

Code Letters
MD

Middle East
Sept 42 to June 45

Operational bases:
Holme on Spalding Moor
8/41 -3/42
Shallufa 9/42 - 3/43
LG91 3/43 - 6/43
Protville 6/43 - 10/43
Bone 10/43 5/44
Alghero 5/44 - 9/44
Foggia 9/44 - 1/45
Gibraltar 1/45 - 6/45
Disbanded

Points of interest

Originally formed as a bomber unit with No.1 Group at Holme on Spalding Moor in August 1941, the squadron's stay with Bomber Command was short-lived, transferring to the Middle East in January 1942. On arrival in Malta during transit, the unit's personnel were absorbed into other units and the squadron did not reform properly until September 1942, when it began operations in the torpedo bomber and general reconnaissance roles.

Wellington MkXIII of 458 Squadron warming-up its engines at Gambut, 1943. This aircraft displays yet another variation on the standard camouflage scheme, this type with the wave pattern extended to the outer leading edge of the wings.

Centre: Wellington IV Z1400 UV-T of 460 Squadron at Breighton in 1942.

P/O J.H.Cameron, from Warialda, Australia, is a picture of concentration at the controls of his 466 Squadron Wellington. Above his right shoulder can be seen the padded leather pilot's seat, a legacy of the pre-WW2 era design. One of the very few concessions to comfort anywhere on the aircraft, Wellington pilots converting to other types often bemoaned the loss of this little bit of luxury.

460

SQUADRON
(Australian)
Bomber Command
Nov 41 to Aug 42
Code Letters
UV

Operational bases:
Molesworth 11/41 - 1/42
Breighton 1/42 - 8/42
Re-equipped with Halifaxes

466

SQUADRON
(Australian)
Bomber Command
Oct 42 to Dec 42
Code Letters
HD

Operational bases:
Driffield 10/42- 12/42
Leconfield 12/42
Re-equipped with Halifaxes

524
SQUADRON
Coastal Command
Apr 44 to May 45

Code Letters
7R

Operational bases:
Davidstowe Moor
4/44 - 7/44
Docking 7/44
Bircham Newton
7/44 - 11/44
Langham 11/44 - 5/45
Disbanded

527
SQUADRON
Radar Testing
Apr 45 to Apr 46

Code Letters
WN

Operational bases:
Digby 4/44 - 11/45
Watton 11/45 - 4/46
Re-equipped with Dominies

544
SQUADRON
Photo Recce
Oct 42 to Dec 45

Code Letters
No Code

Operational bases:
Benson 10/42 - 10/45

524 Squadron was tasked with patrolling for E-boats off the French and later the Dutch and German coasts. Once located, the targets would be illuminated and Strike Wing Beaufighters would be directed into the attack. This photo shows armourers loading drip flares onto racks ready to load into the ship-finding Wellington behind, December 1944.

547

SQUADRON
Coastal Command
Oct 42 to Jan 44

Code Letters
No Code

Operational bases:
Holmsley South
10/42 - 12/42
Chivenor 12/42 - 1/43
Tain 1/43 - 3/43
Chivenor 3/43 - 5/43
Davidstowe Moor
5/43 - 10/43
Thorney Island
10/43 1/44
Re-equipped with
Liberators

Above: NC828 'H' of 621 Squadron sitting in the sun at Khormaksar, May 1945.

Right: MF964 'N' of 621 Squadron flown by W/O Cooper en route to Salalah-Khormaksar, Aden, 14th February 1945.

612

SQUADRON
Coastal Command
Sept 42 to July 45

Code Letters
3
WL
8W

Operational bases:
Wick 9/42 - 4/43
Davidstowe Moor
4/43 - 5/43
Chivenor 5/43 - 11/43
St. Eval 11/43 - 12/43
Chivenor 12/43 - 9/44
Limavady 9/44 - 12/44
Langham 12/44 - 7/45
Disbanded

Below: Wellington GRXIV NB972 8W-M of 612 Squadron in early 1945.

621

SQUADRON
India
Sept 43 to Nov 45

Middle East
Nov 45 to Apr 46

Code Letters
No Code

Operational bases:
Port Reitz 9/43 - 11/43
Mogadishu 11/43 - 12/43
Khormaksar
12/43 - 11/45

Mersa Matruh
11/45 - 4/46
Re-equipped with
Warwicks

Above: W/O Holloway (2nd from left) and crew with their Wellington GRXIV at Kormaksar, 1945. This aircraft has been modified locally by the installation of two .303 machine guns in the nose glazing. Tragically, this crew went missing on the 6th November 1945 during the transit from Aden to Egypt, where the squadron was to take up air-sea rescue duties following the end of hostilities.

Below: W/O Bill Cooper's crew beneath the Hercules XVII engine that powered the Wellington GRXIV. From left to right: F/Sgt E E Woodhouse (Navigator); W/O Bill Cooper (pilot); Sgt Bob Clarke (2nd pilot); and Sgt Robson (Signaller). Producing 1,735 hp, the Hercules XVII was the highest rated engine to power the Wellington.

Above: With his fore'n aft cap at an outrageously rakish angle, Sgt Robson (far left) of Bill Cooper's crew poses with fellow signallers Sgts Waring and Parr by the tail turret of their Wellington. Khormaksar, 1945.

Strictly unofficial squadron crest, the subtleties of which are now lost in time. The official squadron crest, a partly coiled Spitting Cobra snake, is accompanied by the motto "Ever ready to strike".

They also served

Above: A rare bird indeed, Wellington Mkla P2521 MA-V of 161 Squadron, (an ex-DWI aircraft), photographed at Tempsford in the summer of 1942. At the time she was involved in SIS wireless missions.

Right: Another rare photo, this time showing a Wellington Ic T2874 'W' of the Malta Wellington Flight at Luqa in 1940.

Below: Wellington HZ470 'B' of 765 Squadron Fleet Air Arm roaring towards the camera.

OTUs
and other units

Rear turret of 11 OTU Wellington TX-T

Wellington Ia N2887 of the Central Gunnery School with a Mustang and Spitfire, no doubt intent on 'shooting it down'!

9X-S of 1689 Flight, note the thick white code letters

Veteran MkI L4228 (nearest camera) after flying operationally was transferred to the ATA for pilot training.

A crew pose with their Wellington at 10 OTU at Abingdon with ZG-P in the background.

Below: A 9 OTU Wellington receives thorough maintenance in a hangar by female personnel, Gosport 1942.

Below: Squadron Leader W A Smith in the cockpit of a Wellington of 22 OTU at Wellesbourne Mountford.

Wreckage of Z8807 carrying the KJ codes of 11 OTU is inspected by German troops after a forced landing on the continent, August 1941.

Background: This larger photo of N2887 of the CGS shows nicely the wear and tear that the fabric covered Wimpey displayed after a few years of service.

German troops inspect the wreck of DV439 PP-D of 25 OTU on 1st August 1942. This aircraft was shot down by the legendary ace Heinz Wolgang Schnaufer, becoming the second of his 121 victories.

Wellington R1090 ED-K of 21 OTU Moreton-in-Marsh lies in a field after a forced landing.

Above: A Wellington Ic of 76 OTU in the desert.

Left: A 20 OTU Wellington JM-R photographed from inside the fuselage of another Wellington.

OTUs operated a large number of aircraft and frequently had a number of different unit codes. 20 OTU had several including AI, HJ, JM, MK, XL, YR and ZT.

Below: Wellington AI-Q of 20 OTU is refuelled in the Scottish winter snow at Lossiemouth, 1944.

NB813 FMB-O is a T10 of 201 AFS at Swinderby, post-war.

Wellington T10 PG262 FFK-H, of 5 ANS (Air Navigational School) again post-war.

Right: BOAC Wellington BAW1 with ENSA party at El Adem.

Below Right: BAW1 viewed from the port side.

Below: Close up of the nose of a BOAC operated Wellington BAW3.

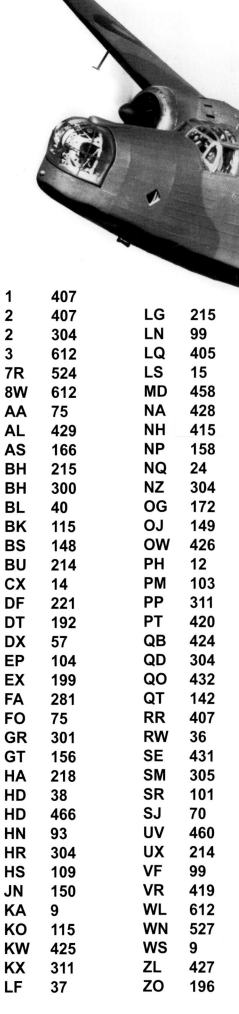

Squadron Codes

1	407		
2	407	LG	215
2	304	LN	99
3	612	LQ	405
7R	524	LS	15
8W	612	MD	458
AA	75	NA	428
AL	429	NH	415
AS	166	NP	158
BH	215	NQ	24
BH	300	NZ	304
BL	40	OG	172
BK	115	OJ	149
BS	148	OW	426
BU	214	PH	12
CX	14	PM	103
DF	221	PP	311
DT	192	PT	420
DX	57	QB	424
EP	104	QD	304
EX	199	QO	432
FA	281	QT	142
FO	75	RR	407
GR	301	RW	36
GT	156	SE	431
HA	218	SM	305
HD	38	SR	101
HD	466	SJ	70
HN	93	UV	460
HR	304	UX	214
HS	109	VF	99
JN	150	VR	419
KA	9	WL	612
KO	115	WN	527
KW	425	WS	9
KX	311	ZL	427
LF	37	ZO	196

The famous R-Robert, N2980, recovered from Loch Ness. A veteran of the disastrous 'Battle of the Heligoland Bight' of 18 December 1939 when 12 of the 22 Wellingtons sent to attack Wilhelmshaven were lost and three more damaged beyond repair. N2980 was with 149 Squadron at the time, but later flew with 37 Squadron before being retired to 20 OTU at Lossiemouth. On December 31st 1940 Squadron Leader Marwood-Elton got into difficulties on a navigation exercise and ordered his six trainees to bale out. He successfully ditched the Wellington in Loch Ness and came ashore in the dinghy with his co-pilot.
The aircraft now rests at Brooklands, Weybridge, where many Wellingtons were made and has been largely restored. Of the 11,461 built it is the only surviving Wellington to have seen operational service, the RAF museum's example being a T10 trainer.

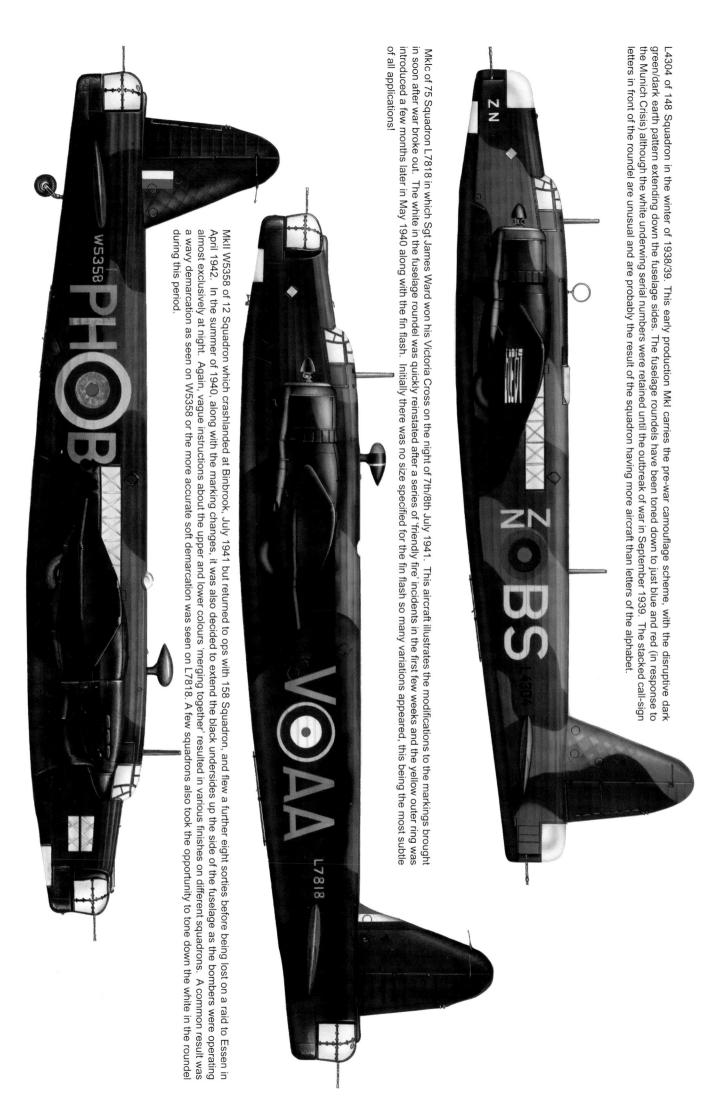

L4304 of 148 Squadron in the winter of 1938/39. This early production MkI carries the pre-war camouflage scheme, with the disruptive dark green/dark earth pattern extending down the fuselage sides. The fuselage roundels have been toned down to just blue and red (in response to the Munich Crisis) although the white underwing serial numbers were retained until the outbreak of war in September 1939. The stacked call-sign letters in front of the roundel are unusual and are probably the result of the squadron having more aircraft than letters of the alphabet.

MkIc of 75 Squadron L7818 in which Sgt James Ward won his Victoria Cross on the night of 7th/8th July 1941. This aircraft illustrates the modifications to the markings brought in soon after war broke out. The white in the fuselage roundel was quickly reinstated after a series of 'friendly fire' incidents in the first few weeks and the yellow outer ring was introduced a few months later in May 1940 along with the fin flash. Initially there was no size specified for the fin flash so many variations appeared, this being the most subtle of all applications!

MkII W5358 of 12 Squadron which crashlanded at Binbrook, July 1941 but returned to ops with 158 Squadron, and flew a further eight sorties before being lost on a raid to Essen in April 1942. In the summer of 1940, along with the marking changes, it was also decided to extend the black undersides up the side of the fuselage as the bombers were operating almost exclusively at night. Again, vague instructions about the upper and lower colours 'merging together' resulted in various finishes on different squadrons. A common result was a wavy demarcation as seen on W5358 or the more accurate soft demarcation was seen on L7818. A few squadrons also took the opportunity to tone down the white in the roundel during this period.

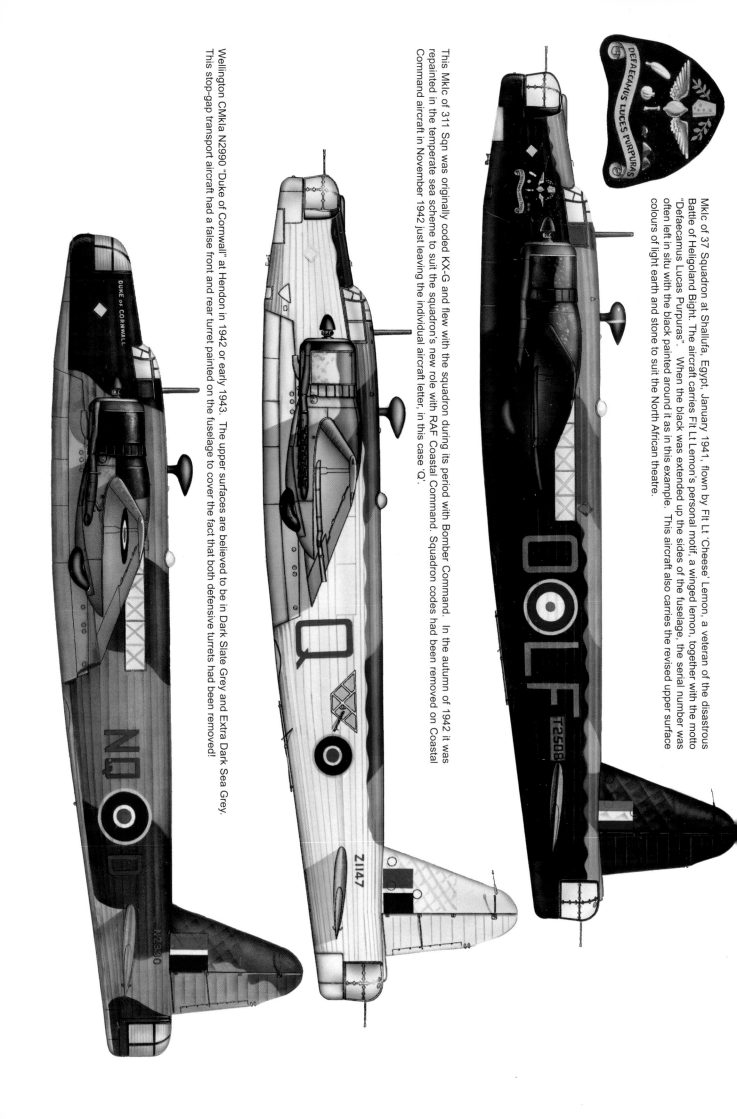

MkIc of 37 Squadron at Shallufa, Egypt, January 1941, flown by Flt Lt 'Cheese' Lemon, a veteran of the disastrous Battle of Heligoland Bight. The aircraft carries Flt Lt Lemon's personal motif, a winged lemon, together with the motto "Defaecamus Lucas Purpuras". When the black was extended up the sides of the fuselage, the serial number was often left in situ with the black painted around it as in this example. This aircraft also carries the revised upper surface colours of light earth and stone to suit the North African theatre.

This MkIc of 311 Sqn was originally coded KX-G and flew with the squadron during its period with Bomber Command. In the autumn of 1942 it was repainted in the temperate sea scheme to suit the squadron's new role with RAF Coastal Command. Squadron codes had been removed on Coastal Command aircraft in November 1942 just leaving the individual aircraft letter, in this case 'Q'.

Wellington CMkIa N2990 "Duke of Cornwall" at Hendon in 1942 or early 1943. The upper surfaces are believed to be in Dark Slate Grey and Extra Dark Sea Grey. This stop-gap transport aircraft had a false front and rear turret painted on the fuselage to cover the fact that both defensive turrets had been removed!

MkIc P9226 of 311 Squadron's training flight. East Wretham in late 1940. Again the wavy demarcation appears on the fuselage and again the white of the roundel has been comprehensively toned down with black. An order issued in September at last defined the size of the fin flash as being stripes of 8 inches wide and 27 inches high.

MkIII Z1572 of 419 ("Moose") Squadron typifies the later appearance of Bomber Command Wellingtons from mid-1942. In an effort to tone down the markings further, the code letters and serial number were repainted in dull red and the fuselage roundel and fin flash were modified to reduce the amount of conspicuous yellow and white. The camouflage demarcation was also resolved into being a solid line at about cockpit level, this being applied at the factory.

MkX HZ950 of 99 (Madras Presidency) Squadron in Burma, 1944. Early experiences in the Far East led to the Allies dropping any form of red in their roundels to avoid mis-identification with the Japanese all red roundels. At first the red was simply removed but a new version of dark blue and pale blue was eventually standardised across the theatre.

MkXIII MF639 of 415 Squadron RAF Coastal Command at Bircham Newton in May 1944. With the squadron operating against German E-boats mainly at night, the Bomber Command night bomber scheme was deemed more appropriate.

MkXIV NB772 of 179 Sqn at Predannack, summer 1944. Coastal Command patrol aircraft were rarely seen with 'invasion stripes' as their operational areas were usually far removed from the Normandy coast. However, this aircraft was involved in Operation Cork at the western end of the English Channel making the carrying of these quick identification markings mandatory.

Wellington MkXIII NC580 of No.69 Squadron, operating in a specialised reconnaissance/illumination role with the 2nd Tactical Air Force out of Melsbroek, Belgium in late 1944. The aircraft wears the night fighter camouflage scheme commonly seen on the Mosquito and Beaufighter intruders at the time.